Advice from the Dean

A Personal Perspective on the Philosophy, Roles, and Approaches of a Dean at a Small, Private, Liberal Arts College

JAMES S. TEDERMAN

Reed College

National Association of Student
Personnel Administrators, Inc.

Additional copies of this monograph may be purchased by contacting NASPA at 1875 Connecticut Avenue, NW, Suite 418, Washington, D.C. 20009-5728; 202-265-7500 (tel.) or 202-797-1157 (fax).

Library of Congress
Cataloging-in-Publication Data
Tederman, James S.
    Advice from the dean : a personal perspective on the philosophy, roles, and approaches of a dean at a small, private liberal arts college / James S. Tederman.
    p. cm.
    Includes bibliographic references (p. 113).
    ISBN 0-931654-22-X
    1. Deans (Education) — United States. 2. Small colleges — United States. 3. Student affairs services — United States. I. Title.
    LB2341.T33 1997   97-22586
    378.1'12—dc21   CIP

Monograph Series Editorial Board
1997-98

Other NASPA Monograph Titles

A Student Affairs Guide to the ADA and Disability Issues

Different Voices: Gender and Perspective in Student Affairs Administration

Diversity, Disunity, and Campus Community

Working with International Students and Scholars on American Campuses

Puzzles and Pieces in Wonderland: The Promise and Practice of Student Affairs Research

The Role of Student Affairs in Institution-Wide Enrollment Management Strategies

The Invisible Leaders: Student Affairs Mid-Managers

The New Professional: A Resource Guide for New Student Affairs Professionals and Their Supervisors

From Survival to Success: Promoting Minority Student Retention

Student Affairs and Campus Dissent: Reflection of the Past and Challenge for the Future

Contents

Contents, cont'd.

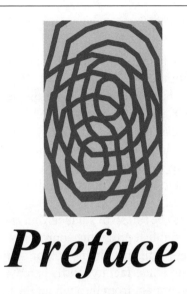

Preface

This monograph is written for the deans of students of small, private, liberal arts colleges; for those who aspire to the position; as well as for presidents, trustees, members of search committees, and others who need to understand the demands and the rewards of student affairs programs.

I have served as dean of students at Grinnell College in Grinnell, Iowa, for 16 years and as dean of students at Western State College in Gunnison, Colorado, for a year. For six years, I have been vice president and dean of student services at Reed College in Portland, Oregon.

I am writing this monograph in part because of my frustration with the lack of good, practical written materials on the role and function of liberal arts college student affairs administrators and the unique challenges and problems faced by deans of students.

I have also written this monograph out of concern over the paucity of material relating to small liberal arts colleges available for use in student affairs graduate programs. Although the majority of practicing professionals in student affairs are employed at small colleges, nearly all graduate programs in the field are located in large universities, mostly public, and are staffed by faculty members whose primary experience is in large institutions. A need exists in graduate training for more materials directly related to small, liberal arts colleges.

This publication is, intentionally, *not a scholarly review* of current practice in the field. It is a monograph by a long-time practitioner at small, private, residential, liberal arts colleges serving traditional-aged full-time students, and is written for fellow practitioners. The professional practices in student affairs at such small, private, liberal arts colleges differ somewhat from public institutions.

The monograph is meant to encourage the new dean of students to think before acting. In strongly expressing my opinions, I have tried to challenge beliefs and assumptions and thereby to help administrators sort out their thoughts in a field where diverse opinions abound about how the job should be done. The monograph is a practical handbook for new deans of students, organized in terms of the major areas they will supervise and the major challenges they will face. It is not intended to provide a program of instruction on how to be a dean of students, but is meant to act as a guide that can help deans establish programs appropriate for their own institutions. The predominant influence on the author's thinking has been years of experience with students, faculty, staff, parents, trustees, and fellow student affairs administrators from throughout the country.

One of the things that makes student affairs practice in liberal arts colleges interesting is the highly diverse nature of the institutions. The personalities of presidents and deans, the religious affiliation of the college or lack of it, the presence or absence of Greek organizations, the size of the endowment, and the demographics of the student body all have a tremendous affect on the philosophy and practice of a student affairs program. This diversity, however, can present problems for anyone attempting to write about the role of dean of students at such institutions, and this may account for lack of materials on the subject.

I have organized the chapters of the monograph so they can be read separately but, as any experienced dean knows, the many parts of the job ultimately cannot be separated from each other. For this reason, I have tried to make the monograph as comprehensive as possible and recommend that it first be read in its entirety.

In Part I, I describe the role of the dean of students, the necessity of formulating a clear program philosophy, and the institutional context, involving students, faculty, and parents, in which the dean works. In particular, I discuss in some detail how I work with students.

In Part II, I explain both the offices and programs the dean of students normally supervises and the other offices of the college with which the dean works on a regular basis. I cover the hiring, supervision, and evaluation of staff. The primary emphasis is on a discussion of each of the student affairs offices and the particular challenges and problems they face in the small liberal arts college environment.

In Part III, I consider several organizational issues affecting the dean of students, including the dean's place in the organizational hierarchy and his or her relationship to the president's cabinet, the board of trustees, and major college committees. Particular attention is given to the ways each of these groups functions within the small college and how the dean of students can work most effectively with them. The renovation of student services buildings is also covered in some detail. Part III ends with advice to new deans of students, including special advice for those who take on the role directly after having served on the faculty.

Acknowledgments

While there are too many to mention by name, I would like to acknowledge and thank all of the staff members who have worked for and with me over the past 25 years. More than anyone else they inspired me to write this manuscript.

I would like to thank Grinnell College, which gave me my start in the field by appointing me resident director, and Wally Walker, past executive vice president and provost of Grinnell College, who was foolish enough to make me dean of students while I was in my late 20s. I would like to thank Liz Abernethy for the assistance she has given me in preparing this manuscript.

I would like to give a special acknowledgment and thanks to my wife, Jane Tederman, who lived with me and our infant son in the residence halls for three years, who has been awaken by all of the late night and early morning telephone calls of the past 25 years, who accompanied me to all of the many functions I attended in my capacity as dean, and who constantly listened to my problems and hopes, giving me excellent advice in many difficult circumstances.

Part I:
CONTEXT

Tremendous changes have occurred in higher education in the last 30 years, nowhere more evidently than in student affairs, an area which has assumed almost the entire responsibility for working with students outside of the classroom. The other great change has been the level of involvement and authority that students have been given over cocurricular programs. Thirty years ago, the social life of students, most particularly the regulations governing it, was largely in the hands of the faculty and faculty committees. Nearly all student organizations and living units had an active faculty adviser. Many, if not most, of the deans of students came directly from the faculty, and, at least in small liberal arts colleges, most had the authority to dismiss a student from school without any formal hearing or guarantee of due process.

Then came the revolution. In the late 1960s and early 1970s, there was a rapid shift from faculty to student and professional staff responsibility for student life. By the mid-1970s, on most college campuses, the faculty had little involvement in student life, except for token representation on committees. In fact, many faculty members were pleased to relinquish this particular responsibility.

It is no coincidence that the faculty retreated from substantial student involvement at the same time that the student affairs staff assumed a larger

1

role on the campus. A vacuum was created which had to be filled, especially as students demanded a greater voice on issues such as drugs, alcohol, coed residence halls, visitation hours, and other concerns. The changes in these areas had a great influence on the role of the dean of students and on the type of skills and abilities the dean needed to successfully fulfill the role.

ROLE OF THE DEAN OF STUDENTS

Today, deans have little or no unilateral authority. Nearly every policy or action must either go through a committee or be approved by one or more committees. These committees are no longer rubber-stamp bodies composed of faculty and fellow administrators; in many instances, students are in the majority. The democratization of student life on small college campuses has gone far beyond any analogous change that has occurred on the academic side.

The role for the dean of students now requires a sophisticated set of skills. Looking back, my own role has become much more complicated in the past 30 years. I no longer have a small office with an assistant and a secretary, and I am no longer able to dispense justice with the stroke of a pen. I am responsible for complicated administrative systems and spend a considerable amount of my time hiring, training, and supervising staff. I must persuade and influence students, rather than just dictating what they must do.

As a dean, I must accept the fact that I am the one who will be held responsible and accountable for student affairs programs. If things go wrong, *I* will have the responsibility for sorting the situation out, even though I was not directly involved in creating the problem. As a dean, I am expected to be concerned about the long-term interests of the students and the college and not to sacrifice them for short-term gains. I am expected to be able to work effectively with and establish confidence in the student affairs programs among students, faculty, administrators, trustees, alumni, parents, and members of the local community. I am expected to recruit, hire, and supervise all the student affairs staff and to be accountable for their professional performance. I am expected to make the student affairs program compatible with and supportive of the academic goals of the college.

This is an impressive list of expectations. The crucial question is, "How does one go about carrying out the role?" Unfortunately, there are no simple rules to follow. There are a few things, however, that must be done well and a few qualities that are essential for a dean's success:

■ The dean of students must, above all, be a person who believes in and is capable of using influence and persuasion rather than relying on unilateral authority. Among the skills and characteristics this requires, the most important ones are: patience, the ability to communicate in speech and writing, knowledge of individual and group behavior, a facility for quickly diagnosing complex social and structural problems, an ability to admit mistakes, and a strong sense of self-confidence. Ultimately, the dean of students' only real power is an ability to persuade and influence, and this requires being trusted by all campus constituents. Gaining this trust is in itself a demanding task.

■ In addition to personality attributes, the dean must function in certain specific roles. The most important by far involves articulating and implementing a comprehensive and easily understood philosophy of student affairs that complements and enhances the particular role and mission of the institution. This, perhaps, is more difficult than it sounds. One cannot just impose the current body of accepted practice upon a college, without taking into account its uniqueness, its particular role and mission. A philosophy appropriate for an independent liberal arts college may not be appropriate for one with a strong religious affiliation.

Due to these differences, student affairs must tailor its roles, missions, and implementation of appropriate policies to each unique educational context. A thorough knowledge of the institution, an understanding of its history and traditions, and of its faculty, students, alumni, and trustees is essential to fulfilling the role of dean. For a student affairs program to work, all of the primary constituencies in the institution must believe in and understand its mission. If this is to occur, the dean of students must be willing and able to hear out and respond to those who offer constructive criticism and those who disagree; the dean must finely hone his or her skills of persuasion and influence if the programs are to live up to their potential.

■ Whatever administrative system is developed, it must be able to meet its stated goals and accomplish the missions using the limited resources that are available.

■ The dean must earn the respect of others in the institution if resources adequate to carrying out the student affairs program are to be made available. Because student affairs programs are often given a low priority, this becomes especially crucial when resources are scarce. In any event, the dean must be a creative manager who achieves the greatest gain with limited means.

■ The dean must also have an ability to hire the very best people and to provide them with the supervision and support necessary for their professional success. Student affairs is a labor-intensive field, and a good staff will determine the success or failure of a program.

■ The dean must constantly seek out and listen to the advice and counsel of staff members and others who may be close to situations that arise and must balance their opinions against his or her own knowledge, experience, and the long-term interests of the institution. The dean must constantly be open to new approaches to old problems.

■ A dean must adhere to the highest standards of honesty in his or her dealings with others. A significant aspect of the job is to set appropriate standards of behavior for students and hold them responsible for their behavior. It is not possible to do this effectively unless the dean's own behavior is exemplary. Again, to be effective the dean must earn the respect of students, faculty, and fellow administrators.

■ The dean must be committed not only to student affairs but also to the institution. Student affairs programs at small colleges often experience a high turnover among deans of students. This is unfortunate insofar as it takes many years to develop and build a strong program and today too few deans remain at an institution long enough to carry the process through.

■ If the dean is to survive, he or she must cultivate a good sense of humor and an understanding and tolerance for the often irrational behavior of human beings.

Two factors that have a crucial impact on the success of a dean are the development of a clear, simple, and coherent program philosophy, which can be readily understood by everyone, and the recruitment, training, and supervision of excellent staff. When the dean is able to articulate goals clearly and has a staff capable of implementing them, there is a good chance for success.

Anyone considering taking on a dean of students position at a small, private, liberal arts college campus should seriously consider the demands that will be made: very direct involvement in the day-to-day operation of the student affairs program; willingness to go to the campus late at night and on weekends, helping with suicidal, psychotic, and disruptive students; attendance at student social events that may potentially lead to problems; and direct involvement in almost every kind of emergency that takes place on the campus. For all practical purposes, a dean is on call 24 hours a day, seven days a week, whenever the college is in session. It is a demanding position with a great deal of stress.

Added to the demands of the position is the difficulty of finding people who can give advice and support, who can serve as trusted colleagues. Because the higher administrative levels of many institutions are still dominated by males, this may be especially difficult for a woman who prefers the advice of another woman. The dean will be called upon to make many very difficult and controversial decisions about policy, students, and staff. Because so many decisions involve gray areas where there is no clear-cut solution, I have found myself open to second guessing by others on campus, and at a small college where everyone knows everyone else, such criticism often has a very personal edge. This can make the dean's position an extremely lonely one, and I have found that the confidence of a colleague whose judgment is sound and who can be trusted absolutely to be an invaluable asset.

Although some use fellow deans from other institutions to fill this role, someone from another college may lack the necessary deep understanding of the nuances of one's own institution to act as a reliable sounding board. I have had best success by carefully seeking out a colleague on my own campus. In some fortunate cases, the trusted colleague has been my supervisor, although such an arrangement has the potential to cause problems. It may not always be advisable to express one's innermost doubts, fears, and hesitations to a supervisor, who might seek to relieve those concerns by presenting a solution with which one may ultimately disagree. It often takes time to find someone whose judgment and confidentiality can be trusted. It is better not to rush, but first to try to get to know as many people as possible. Members of the faculty can often be trusted colleagues, especially if they have a good knowledge of the institution and an understanding of administrative processes. What I look for more than anything else is a wise friend, someone who will listen to my problems but not assume responsibility for them, and who will constructively challenge and criticize my thinking.

I have mentioned several times the necessity for the dean of students to win respect and influence, both personally and for the student affairs programs. This is not always a simple process, and it usually can only be done slowly, over several years, which is a primary reason why deans benefit from remaining at their positions for extended periods of time. Many students and faculty members have an anti-authoritarian streak that causes them to distrust administrators and even to treat the dean with a degree of disdain. This should not be taken personally, at least initially, because it is directed toward the administrative position, not the person who holds it. Respect from and influence with the faculty and students are the results of exhibiting honesty and sincerity in relationships with others; showing commitment, concern, and knowledge of the institution; and demonstrating competence in situations that demand that good decisions be made and be carried out effectively.

It is often necessary to prove to students and faculty members that student affairs programs can improve students' ability to take advantage of the college's educational programs. Although we in student affairs are very aware of how student life outside the classroom has a dramatic impact on academic success, faculty members do not always see this connection. The only way to make the point and to gain respect for the value of good student affairs programs is by actually helping students to succeed academically.

Many small college deans now also assume the role of vice president. Often this means that the dean supervises such areas as financial aid, admissions, and even athletics, in addition to student affairs, vastly complicating and significantly changing the role of the dean of students. The vice president and dean of student affairs' role is to provide, in consultation with the president, the faculty, and the students, leadership and direction to the non-academic programs and services of the college, with the general goal of helping to create an environment that allows students to take full advantage of the college's academic programs.

The dual role of vice president and dean can be problematic if it is expected that a single person will fulfill the hands-on, one-to-one duties of adviser and counselor to students, supervise student affairs staff members, manage major parts of the college's programs, participate as a senior officer of the college in institution-wide decisions and initiatives, and help to represent the college to outside constituents. The often unhappy result of this is that the dean of students is expected to fulfill both the old role of counselor, friend, and confidant for students, and the new role of supervisor of a large professional staff and manager of major programs of the college. The changes often occur over the course of many years, without the leaders of the institution understanding the implications, and many small college deans have spoken with me about the great difficulty they have had in performing all of these roles. As the role has grown far beyond what can be expected of any one person, some deans have performed poorly or failed. This growth and change in expectations thus demands attention as a potential problem that must be confronted by any new dean.

PROGRAM PHILOSOPHY

I have stressed the importance of the development of a program philosophy by the dean of students because I believe that a primary reason student affairs programs are often inadequately supported is that their purpose and their importance to the institution's mission is misunderstood. Part of the reason for this is that student affairs administrators have not always done a convincing job of explaining their programs to students, faculty, and staff. On my own campus, I never miss an opportunity to explain my program and its significance to the faculty, the president, and to all constituents. Taking full advantage of these opportunities is difficult unless one has articulated a coherent and easily understood philosophy beforehand and devised the means of implementing that philosophy.

In developing, explaining, and implementing my personal student affairs philosophy, I have kept the following principles in mind:

■ Make sure the philosophical principles are sensitive to and directly support the academic programs of the college and its traditions and mission and make these connections explicit.

■ Keep it simple. The idea is to have people come to believe in, or at least accept, the philosophy and to keep it in mind. Even in institutions of higher education, people do not always take the time to understand and remember a complicated concept. This does not mean that the philosophy should be superficial or not based upon the very best thinking and research in the field, but this research and thought must be distilled into easily understood basic concepts. There will, however, be times, particularly in meetings with the faculty, when a dean of students will have to articulate the philosophy in greater detail, and to support and defend it with reference to current research.

■ Write the philosophy down and distribute it widely — in the college catalogue, the student handbook, staff handbooks, student staff handbooks, parent handbooks, as well as in smaller publications such as judicial council and student organization guidelines. By constant repetition, verbal and written, it will become part of the language of the institution.

■ Always refer to the means of carrying out the philosophy at the same time that the philosophy itself is presented. If the ends are not associated with practical means for achieving them, the philosophy will be seen as a hollow shell.

■ Remember that it takes time for a student affairs philosophy to be developed and accepted by the institution. If an institution does not have a publicly understood and well-accepted student affairs philosophy, expect it to take at least four to eight years to develop one.

The most important single element of the student affairs philosophy is the explanation of how the programs directly support the students' academic success. Too many student affairs programs have moved away from this central institutional goal, and some programs have established cocurricular programs that appear to have little direct relationship to it, a point well discussed in Bloland, Stamatakos, and Rogers' *Reform in Student Affairs* (1994); whether or not one agrees with the authors' conclusions, this thought-provoking publication raises fundamental issues about the role of student affairs in higher education. Also valuable is *Involving Colleges* by Kuh, Schuh, Whitt, and Associates (1991), which thoroughly illustrates the essential elements of several good student programs.

A well-developed philosophy of student affairs is a crucial factor in developing a program of excellence. It can help the institution achieve such excellence, however, only if it does not gather dust in the dean's file cabinet. It must be a working document that acts as an integral part of all aspects of the student affairs program. Use it in staff training, reinforce it in staff meetings, and apply it to the situations that staff members confront in their day-to-day work with students. Its basic premises should be repeated at every opportunity and used as a benchmark against which professional staff, student staff, programs, and offices are evaluated. For example, all end-of-the-year reports by directors of units should be based upon how well the unit has (or has not) carried out the philosophy of the student affairs division. All individual staff evaluations should also measure how well the staff member has furthered the program philosophy. It should be a living document that can be challenged and changed if proven to be wrong or ineffective.

To function as such a living document, the program philosophy must be backed up by an administrative structure and staff that can implement its principles. An excellent staff is the most crucial element to a good program, and it is impossible to spend too much time recruiting and retaining the best possible staff members. These staff members must, moreover, work in an effective administrative decision-making structure that allows the proper involvement with and gains the confidence of the key constituents of the college, that ensures that decisions and policies will be made in a rational, considered, and efficient manner that does not needlessly frustrate participants.

We in student affairs have sometimes too readily adopted student development theories without subjecting them to analysis and critique, often leading to the development of cocurricular programs that have little direct relationship to the primary academic purposes of the college. This has often hurt the credibility of the student affairs office with the faculty. Our mission should not be separate from the academic program but directly linked to it. Student affairs programs exist to support the institution's academic program, and our specific philosophies and programs must be evaluated in terms of their success in enabling students to take full advantage of the academic programs.

STUDENTS

The title of this section is, perhaps, redundant, insofar as most of this monograph is about students and how student affairs administrators work with them. This section, however, makes some general comments about students and goes on to discuss some particular types of students with whom deans spend a disproportionate amount of their time. Once again, I remind the reader that the students with whom I am primarily concerned are of traditional college age and that they attend small, private, liberal arts colleges.

Although students provide the reason for the existence of colleges and are among the most exciting and challenging of people, at one time or another almost every dean of students has said, deep in his or her soul, "Colleges would be great places to work if only there were no students." Still, contact with students is what ultimately makes life as a dean of students so satisfying. Students have kept me young and they have made me old; they are creative, demanding, and frustrating in ways that challenge me and force me to learn. Throughout the years, students have questioned nearly every basic belief, both personal and professional, that I hold near and dear. My beliefs have not been unexamined ones because students have not allowed them to be. Students are ultimately what makes what we do worthwhile.

Some people claim that student affairs is a young person's profession, citing both the age of students and their rapidly changing styles and interests. My many years in the profession, however, lead me to dispute this claim. The age of the person working with students is not as critical as his or her attitudes and knowledge. Many of the basic developmental issues students face have not changed very much over the past 20 years, and some of those who are most successful in working with students are much older than those students.

The world has, no doubt, changed. We now must work with many more students who come from broken homes, who are taking psychotropic medication, who have long histories of psychological treatment, who have been diagnosed with learning disabilities, who have been victims of abuse and neglect, or who have parents who are substance abusers. For all the changes, however, the primary developmental struggles of the students have not essentially changed. As in the past, students continue to face and struggle with the vectors of developing competence that are outlined so effectively by Chickering (Chickering & Reisser, 1993): managing emotions, moving through autonomy toward interdependence, developing mature relationships, establishing identity, developing purpose, and developing integrity. What is different today is that many of our students face these developmental issues carrying much more baggage than was typical in the past. While recognizing the constants, an effective dean must also be well informed about the backgrounds typical of today's students.

Our students differ from many of their peers who are facing identical developmental tasks because they are confronting them within the unique setting of a small college, whose very purpose demands that they search for truth and analyze, criticize, and test all their prior beliefs and assumptions. The focus of this intellectual questioning does not usually remain confined to the classroom and academic topics. What is learned in the classroom is applied to personal life, leading to a unique period of self-examination during which students, especially those in residential settings, place themselves, their family, and their friends under intense scrutiny. It is an exciting and demanding time, but also, at times, one that is quite frightening.

Meeting Basic Student Needs

Along with Chickering's vectors, all student affairs administrators should occasionally dust off and reread Maslow's (1971) analysis of the role of basic human needs as the necessary foundation for the fulfillment of higher needs. Food, housing, and security of self and belongings are not the most exciting of topics for many student affairs administrators and too often they are viewed as necessities that have to be provided so that student affairs staff can get on with the really interesting parts of their jobs, such as educational programming, counseling, workshops, and conferences. We need to be constantly on guard to make certain that we do not neglect the basic physical needs of our students in our rush to work on the interesting parts of our jobs. The quality of a student's daily living environment is extremely important to his or her well-being and to the ability to take advantage of educational opportunities. One of the biggest problems on many campuses that I have visited involves the neglect of this simple fact.

Too many residence halls are suffering from years of deferred maintenance, inadequate bathrooms, poorly designed rooms, and outdated security systems. Too many food services are run more for profit and ease of operation than to provide good and nutritional food. Many dining facilities are drab, noisy, and do little to enhance student interaction. It is difficult, if not impossible, for students who live in such environments to care about each other and their residence halls. The physical environment in which we place students has a tremendous influence on their behavior toward each other and the college. To ignore this basic fact by failing to provide good, not just adequate, living facilities will impair the college's entire educational program.

In times of budgetary constraints (which seem to be perpetual), it is difficult to get presidents, deans, and faculty members very excited about spending funds on the residence halls and food service, but it is the job of the dean of students to do so. We need to be creative, persuasive, and forceful in fighting for funds to accommodate these basic student needs. A good dean of students will always make good living conditions the base upon which the rest of the programs are built. Much time and effort should be spent on fighting for the funds for better heating systems, plumbing, furniture, dining halls, and for the other seemingly mundane improvements that will contribute so much to the development of an effective learning environment.

Helping the Student Who Is Experiencing
Developmental Problems

Nearly all students are going to need or want help with a problem at some time during their college careers. Society has changed a great deal in the last two decades and our students have not been immune from the effects of the changes. I am not referring to the student with pathological problems, but rather the student with developmental problems. Because the period from age 17 to age 21 is accompanied by tremendous change, growth, and development, young adults almost inevitably have problems; those who do not are probably not growing in maturity. At many small colleges, students do not receive the help they need because: (a) they do not know to whom they can turn; (b) they do not recognize that they need help; (c) they do not trust the system which offers help; (d) they do not find the types of assistance they would feel comfortable using available; (e) their need for help is not recognized and help is not offered; and (f) the institutional ethos is not one which encourages them to seek help.

The key to providing effective helping services for students is to create a strong student affairs office which the faculty understands and supports, whose programs are trusted and respected by students who see them as genuinely motivated by a concern for students' welfare and are specifically designed to enhance student academic success. Trust and respect are never just given; they must be earned on a daily basis, one student and faculty member at a time. The good news is, if an office genuinely does care about students and helps them to be academically successful, the word will get out pretty quickly, and students themselves will become the office's most effective advocates.

A residential program is especially beneficial because, if properly organized, all of the common roadblocks to a student's receiving help can be overcome more easily. A strong program will offer many alternative sources of help, starting with trained student staff members — I'll call such students *resident advisers* — who live on the residence hall floor. The resident adviser's primary function is to help the students, and he or she must be perceived as someone who is both genuinely caring and able to keep a confidence.

Good resident advisers become the eyes and ears of a helping program. Friends of students in trouble will come to the advisers seeking advice and consultation, thereby becoming part of the referral system. The resident adviser will also, when appropriate, take an active role by offering help to students who are in obvious difficulty. Because they live with the students, they can play an important preventive role in recognizing problems and effectively getting students help before their problems become overwhelming. The resident adviser thus becomes the essential first link in letting students know that their college cares about them and wishes to help them.

As Astin's (1993) studies have indicated, many students, especially those at small, private, liberal arts colleges, are naturally distrustful of authority, see themselves as being unconventional, and have low scores on internal cohesiveness. New students often equate student affairs administrators with high school principals and disciplinary personnel. As a peer, the resident adviser is often more effective than the professional staff in alleviating student fears and misconceptions about the assistance available at the college and in making an effective referral to sources of help. The key to delivering effective helping services is to gain the trust and the respect of students, and as long as resident advisers believe in the student affairs program, they can act as an effective bridge between the student affairs program and the students.

Those who work in student affairs programs also need a thorough knowledge of human behavior and good counseling skills because they are constantly called upon to help students learn how to take control of their own lives, to make their own decisions, and then live with the consequences. Not a simple process, it requires both knowledge and skill on the part of the staff member as well as the courage to tell students the truth even when it may cause anger and pain.

College students are at a point in their lives when they can no longer afford indulgent self-deception. They often need someone who is willing to be truthful, objective, and supportive, who cares enough not to let them displace responsibility for their own behavior and their own lives, and to help them learn how to take responsibility for themselves. The professional relationship established with students is not always going to be entirely pleasant. It is not the job of the student affairs staff to win the love of the student body. Show me a dean of students that everyone loves and I will show you one who is not doing the job effectively. Neither, however, is a dean of students who is hated by everyone effectively doing the job. Deans should not strive to have all students love them, but they should strive to gain respect through their honesty, fairness, and commitment to student welfare.

Student Behavioral Problems

A major point I want to make in this monograph is on the necessity of creating a program that most students trust and that encourages them to view student affairs programs as helpful resources. To achieve this positive view of student affairs programs while continuing to hold students accountable for unacceptable behavior, the following policies and practices must be instituted:

■ The institution does not assume an *in loco parentis* role, i.e., does not treat its students as children and impose a moral code upon them.

■ The institution holds them accountable for acting as adults.

■ The institution has clear and objective standards of behavior, but only insofar as student behavior has a direct impact on the college's role as an educational and residential community.

A small college must make clear to its students that, aside from a core set of values needed for carrying out its educational mission, its role is to help them, as adults, form their own value systems and beliefs. No college can be value-neutral, particularly those with a religious mission, but even non-sectarian liberal arts colleges have a special burden to demonstrate that their core values are deeply connected to their primary mission. Similarly, residential colleges must show that their rules and regulations are necessary to create and maintain an effective learning community. With its core principles clearly enunciated and placed into practice, the disciplinary role of the dean of students becomes one of helping the community enforce its own version of the social contract, always keeping in mind that the rules serve to allow the college to fulfill its stated mission and are not arbitrarily imposed for the moral good of students.

To see this approach in practice, consider the issue of alcohol consumption in residence halls. I realize the legal requirements governing the use of alcohol by underage students have changed considerably in the past few years and this constrains many institutions' ability to make policy in this area, but I will set out an ideal approach that is not subject to such constraints. Because the consumption of alcohol by those under the age of 21 is illegal in all states, and because most resident students are under 21, many institutions have completely prohibited the possession and consumption of alcohol in the residence halls, with the enforcement of the rule placed in the hands of the professional and student staff in the residence halls. According to the Core Alcohol and Drug Surveys conducted by deans at selective liberal arts colleges, between 60 and 90 percent of college students consume alcohol in spite of the regulations, putting the residence hall staff in the position of enforcing a regulation that almost everyone ignores. This forces the student staff members who live in the hall to play a cat-and-mouse game with their fellow students, perhaps leading them to be perceived as enemies and as spies of the administration. Often no longer welcome in student rooms, out of fear that they will see a prohibited substance, staff members are treated as if they are a police rather than as young men and women genuinely concerned about student welfare. Thus, taking on the responsibility for the enforcement of state alcohol codes undermines not only the staff's rapport with the residents but also the overall effectiveness of the residence hall program.

Banning alcohol from the campus rarely stops students from drinking, but it often shifts the drinking. The related problems of noise and vandalism move into the community surrounding the campus, making it a police rather than a college community problem, one made all the more serious insofar as it increases the number of students driving after having consumed alcohol. By prohibiting the use of alcohol on campus we thus may lose our ability to work with students to limit the number of kegs available, to assure the availability of alternative beverages and food, and to become aware of abuse and so able to offer assistance to those who develop drinking problems. The prohibition of the use of alcohol on campus may make our jobs in some ways easier, but it does not enable us to help our students learn to cope with a socially accepted drug and the many problems its use can create.

In treating students as adults, does a college have an obligation to strictly enforce the law concerning the possession and consumption of alcohol? In ideal circumstances, I would argue that the college has no obligation in situations where such enforcement does not help foster an effective living and learning environment. The college does have an obligation to inform its students of the law and its penalties and to let them know that it will not provide legal assistance to students who violate the law. The college should also provide students with its own policies concerning alcohol. Although the college also must clearly state that it encourages its students to abide by the law, the students, like young adults off campus, should be allowed to make their own decisions concerning the possession and consumption of alcohol and assume responsibility for the consequences of those decisions. The college's primary concern should be with abuse and with alcohol-related behavioral problems. Although recent federal legislation tends to prohibit this type of policy on many of our campuses, I would argue that the college should grant students the same rights to privacy in their individual rooms which they, as adults, would have in private apartments.

As can be surmised from this example, the policy of treating students as adults and refusing to impose any values on them that are not necessary to carry out the college's educational and residential mission will not end the heated debates over the appropriateness of student regulations. Strong arguments, for example, can be made for and against the institutional prohibition of the possession or consumption of alcohol. The policy would, however, constructively shift the debate from legal and moral concerns to questions of whether the use of alcohol on campus is so detrimental to the living and learning environment that it should be prohibited or regulated. If it is decided that alcohol use should be prohibited, an attempt could be made to devise an enforcement mechanism that would not tend to destroy the overall effectiveness of the residential program.

The philosophy of student conduct I have advocated will, no doubt, be problematic at many church-related colleges. One of the strengths of small colleges is that they can offer prospective students real choices in the type of higher educational and social environment they want to experience, and because of this I would have no objection to any church-related, or other, institution that regulates the conduct and social lives of its students. They must, however, do so openly, and they must practice what they preach. What is objectionable is a college that prescribes norms for student conduct and then looks the other way when it comes to enforcement of the norms. Too many colleges have strict regulations on alcohol and drug use and sexual conduct, but then ignore discreet violations of the rules. Such a lesson in hypocrisy has no place in higher education and eventually causes students to lose respect for the institution.

All deans of students must also face the problem of the use and abuse of illegal drugs by students. The use of illegal substances is, unfortunately, once again on the rise in our grade schools and high schools, and many students are entering college with much longer histories of drug use. This picture is complicated even more by the number of entering students who take prescription drugs as a part of therapy programs; mixing prescription drugs with illegal drugs or alcohol, or both, can be very dangerous. Both preventive and reactive programs must be in place to assist students with drug-related problems.

Preventive programs based on moral or legal premises are not very successful at the college level, so preventive programs should be based on the fact that drug and alcohol use is antithetical to the goal of academic excellence. Increasing scientific evidence, for example, suggests that marijuana use has negative effects on short- and long-term memory and cognitive reasoning (Pope & Yurgelun-Scott, 1996). Because students at small liberal arts colleges tend to have the greatest respect for the opinions of the faculty, faculty members must support preventive programs and send a strong institutional message to the students. Such faculty cooperation is much more likely when a drug and alcohol policy is based on educational, rather than legal or moral, foundations.

If reactive programs are to be successful, they must be centered on concern for the students and on their own interest in the safety of their friends and peers. This requires designing intervention programs whose primary purpose is not disciplinary but, rather, oriented to getting students into appropriate treatment programs, in some cases in conjunction with a medical leave of absence. If students believe that staff members are going to punish their friends rather than help them, they will not come to them for assistance.

Working with students who are having behavioral problems is one of the more challenging and interesting roles in student affairs, especially for the dean of students. Although I have seen countless numbers of problem students in my 25 years in student affairs, rarely has a student come into my office and said, "Yes, I did it. I was wrong. What is the college going to do to me?" When working with problem students, always be prepared to hear some of the most elaborate and creative displacement-of-responsibility stories imaginable. A common ploy is to make offense the best defense. If a student is caught stealing a college chair from a lounge, expect a response such as, "If you folks hadn't picked out such god-awful-colored upholstery, I never would have taken it. I was just trying to do everyone in the hall a favor by getting rid of it. No one likes the chair or wants it in the lounge." Such a student is practicing the old game of turn-the-tables, placing the blame on something or someone else, and trying to put me on the defensive. Some students can be very creative and quite amusing, but if one falls for their ploy, in this case perhaps by being drawn into a discussion of the color of the chair, the culprit will have succeeded in so removing the conversation from the actual problem of honesty that there is a danger of forgetting to return to the issue that is really at stake.

Students can sometimes be so creative that it might be a good use of a dean's time to go to a detective school. Never, however, get so personally caught up in the game that you seek to "get" the student. With the exception of a few students with true antisocial personality disorders, who I will discuss below, most problem students are not all bad and are worth the effort made to reach them. Many are crying out for someone to pay attention to them and to offer them help. Some of the most satisfying experiences and relationships I have had as a dean of students have come from my work with students with behavioral problems, and these are the students who are likely to stop by to see me after graduating.

As a dean, it is best to be realistic with these students, refusing to let them blame everyone and everything else for their problems, drawing clear lines that they will not be allowed to cross, while at the same time also demonstrating compassion and caring. The expression *tough love* fits well here. In the long run, these students have often greatly appreciated the fact that I cared enough to stand up to them. Many times they have spent their lives conning their parents, high school teachers, counselors, and friends. If I fall for the con, they have no respect for me, and my chance of having a positive influence on them is lost. By dealing with them honestly and realistically from the very beginning, I have helped some confused, angry, and frightened students to bloom into young men and women who like and respect themselves. This can be one of the most satisfying and rewarding aspects of the profession.

There are, however, some few exceptions: students who, after careful and considered observation and diagnosis, reveal true antisocial personality disorders. Such students manifest a pervasive pattern of disregard for and violation of the rights of others. Often they appear to be exceptionally charming and sincere, and they may be extremely intelligent. Unfortunately, they are also amoral, capable of doing almost anything they perceive to be in their best interest. A college environment, composed generally of trusting people who believe that reason always wins over evil, is a Garden of Eden for such a student, and he or she can create havoc in such a setting.

These students provide the sole exception to the policy of never seeking to "get" a student. In my experience, neither student affairs nor mental health professionals can work effectively with such students, and an effort should be made to remove them as quickly as possible from the campus. Although such a policy goes against the grain of my belief in allowing students to learn from their mistakes, and, without care, it also may be subject to abuse, I have come to the conclusion that a college must protect itself from those who would prey on it and its students. In dealing with such a student, a dean of students should seek out all the help and consultation available from mental health professionals so that he or she is certain of the diagnosis; but once the diagnosis is certain, the student must be disciplined. Care must be taken to use the same procedural safeguards offered to all students and to base the disciplinary action on proven behavioral incidents, not on a psychological diagnosis.

In general, problem students and problem situations must be viewed as challenges and learning opportunities rather than as headaches. It is perhaps asking too much to expect that such a positive attitude will always be adopted, but without this overall attitude, the job eventually becomes drudgery. Problem students often turn out to be among the brightest of students, and a dean can gain a special satisfaction in helping them live up to their tremendous potential.

Life-Endangering Situations

Like society as a whole, a campus will have its share of seriously disturbed community members. Whether or not the college has a counseling center, the final decision about allowing a severely disturbed student to remain in school and in the residence halls will rightfully fall to the dean of students. Such students present a dean with very difficult decisions. By inclination and profession, student affairs workers seek to teach students how to take control of their own lives, and it is extremely difficult to make the necessary decisions to take control away from a student. A dean must, however, make such decisions quite often.

Every dean of students should read Pavela's *Dismissal of Students with Mental Disorders* (1985), a monograph that offers excellent and thoughtful advice about working with emotionally disturbed students. Pavela, an attorney, outlines the legal rights of the disturbed student and the often conflicting responsibility for protecting the college and its students. Pavela understands the college campus, the role of the dean, and the mental health needs of the disturbed student. He offers holistic advice in an attempt to provide solutions that will benefit both the student and the college within a legal and ethical framework.

Working with suicidal students is a situation where it is better to be safe than sorry. Any type of suicidal behavior must be taken seriously with immediate intervention. Students exhibiting suicidal behavior must be confronted and helped to accept responsibility for their actions. Although this should be done in a positive and caring way, suicidal students can be very uncooperative, manipulative, and angry. An immediate assessment should be made of the student by a mental health professional, although the student will often resist and resent this intrusion and sometimes will refuse to be evaluated.

At times, these students will engage in manipulative behavior, trying to get their way by instilling guilt in their friends for telling me about the attempt. They will get their friends, faculty members, and others to intervene on their behalf, misrepresenting the actions and motivations of those trying to help them in order to prevent intrusions into their lives. In the face of all of this, it is necessary to insist that an assessment be made, even if this involves a threat of an involuntary withdrawal of the student from the college in the form of a medical leave of absence. Similar considerations apply to students who are experiencing severe eating disorders or drug or alcohol problems, who may also resist help and act in a manipulative manner. It is not pleasant to intrude forcefully in the life of another person, and it is not something that should be done lightly or routinely. To be very certain of the facts, the advice and assistance from mental health professionals and legal counsel is required. Once the facts are relatively clear, however, it is important to act immediately and not to back down when faced with resistance.

One student who had attempted suicide by slashing his wrists got extremely angry with me for insisting that unless he had a professional assessment he could not remain at the college. The student argued that it was his life to do with as he pleased and that I had absolutely no business interceding. My response was, "If you lived on the moon, I might agree with you, but you do not live on the moon. You live in the residence halls and your actions have drastically affected the lives of your friends and hallmates. You must take responsibility for what you have done. If you refuse to do so, I will assume the responsibility for you." The student would not talk to me for the rest of the time he was in college and never missed an opportunity to express to others how insensitive, mean, and manipulative I was. Several years after his graduation, however, he contacted me during a college reunion and thanked me for caring enough to stand up to him and save his life. Without a doubt, the intervention, however difficult, was worth the effort.

Colleges should institute "medical leaves of absence" for students who have been professionally diagnosed as having severe medical or psychiatric problems that make it temporarily impossible for them to function in the college environment. The duration of the leave should be open-ended, with the only requirement for a return to the college being a statement by a physician or therapist who has treated the student indicating that he or she is ready and able to return to the campus educational environment, along with an indication of whether the student needs ongoing treatment. The student's therapist should be in direct contact with the college's director of counseling, so there is an opportunity to inform the therapist about the environment into which the student will be returning and the academic and personal demands the student will face. If ongoing treatment is specified, continued enrollment should be made contingent upon receiving the treatment. Deans must assist students to find appropriate help and make sure they realize they are welcome to return to the college as soon as they are ready.

Fear of having an official record of the reason for a leave can be a major roadblock in getting a student to voluntarily accept one, so transcripts should merely state that the student was on a "leave of absence," omitting any mention of the cause of the leave. Except when a student is able to finish his or her courses away from the residence, institutional arrangements should be made for the assignment of a non-punitive W for current courses. When a student leaves late enough in a semester that a professor believes a course can legitimately be completed without the student's continued presence in the classroom, and where there is no medical reason against doing so, institutional arrangements should be made to allow a student to complete course requirements out of residence. I have seen numerous students with severe psychiatric and medical problems take a medical leave of absence and later return to successfully finish their college careers.

Private colleges have a much greater degree of latitude in placing students on medical leaves of absence than do many public institutions. For example, due process may not be required by the college's own policies. Nevertheless, colleges should be very thoughtful in designing and implementing medical leave polices. Legal advice should be sought, particularly with regard to the use of confidential medical and psychological records, since laws concerning such issues can vary from state to state.

Do not make the wrong inference from these comments. As long as a student can perform academically, the first goal should always be to find a way to keep the student in school. Even very ill students are sometimes capable of doing acceptable academic work. Granting extensions for course assignments, obtaining reduced course loads through the dropping of a course(s), tutoring, and referral for intensive therapy provide some means of accomplishing this. Some students experiencing severe problems may have no realistic alternatives to staying at the college. They may no longer have parents who support them, may lose medical insurance once they are no longer enrolled, or may face a non-supportive home environment that will harm them more than if they were to continue at the college. These can be the most difficult of cases, particularly if a student's remaining at the college is disruptive to the lives of other students. Each case must be handled individually, often taking hours and hours of staff time.

Student Demonstrations and Confrontations

Understandably, deans of students and other administrators often react very negatively to student demonstrations, particularly ones that are directed toward them. The mission of a liberal arts college is to help students develop critical and inquiring minds, and we should not be surprised or angered when they use these skills to criticize the college. Students who question, challenge, and even demonstrate for what they believe in are an indication of a healthy liberal arts college. As long as it is handled properly, controversy can be a learning opportunity for students and staff. This is not to deny, however, the discomfort of facing a hostile and angry group of people. Deans better become used to it, however, as student political involvement on our campuses, I hope, will never go away.

There are several things to keep in mind when facing a group of demonstrators or when defending the institution's actions to a meeting of angry students:

■ Do not become angry. Try to remember that most of the anger is not personal but is directed at the action, policy, or condition that is the object of the protest.

■ Garner the facts before entering such a situation. Never make inaccurate statements and never make promises that cannot be kept. As a spokesperson, a dean's credibility and sincerity are the only things that can be used to turn a situation around. Once these assets are compromised, the dean will become totally ineffective.

■ During most protests, administrators and the institution will be accused of having evil motives. Students, and sometimes faculty members, often look for a "smoking gun" behind every administrative action with which they disagree. To overcome this paranoid view of administrators, students must become aware that there can be honest differences of opinion that do not arise from base motives. The best way to teach this is by example. Respect student opinions and try to not react to them on a personal basis. Ask that students show an equal respect for those with whom they disagree.

■ Since many crises are triggered by value-laden, highly emotional issues, it is important to diffuse the emotion and anger, not add to it, to help students to apply reason, logic, and a respect for differing opinions. This is not an easy task, especially if the protestors are extremely angry. It is sometimes impossible to discuss an emotionally charged topic reasonably with a large group of people, especially if some members of the group are more interested in playing to the audience than in addressing the issue. In this situation, I have found it best to take my lumps, stay cool, and immediately set up a small task force to sit down in a calmer environment for a discussion of the issue.

■ Prior to the task force meetings, give some long, hard thought to the issues on the table. Try to determine in advance of the meeting whether there are compromises that could be made without hurting the institution. When dealing in gray areas, where there can be no absolute certainty as to what is right or wrong, do not view compromise as a sign of weakness or incompetence. If you wish students to listen to you, *you* must be able to listen to them. At times, however, no compromise is possible, and a dean has to stick to his or her guns. When I am convinced that what I am doing is right and there is no room for compromise, I listen carefully to the students and defend my position strongly but patiently. Patience is the strongest ally at this point, and one must be willing to calmly and thoroughly answer the same questions over and over again, without showing frustration and anger. At some point, however, the time comes to say, "we will have to agree to disagree," letting the students know they will not be able to convince the administration of the correctness of their position.

■ Prior to the onset of such a crisis, the college and the students must have been informed of what behaviors and actions are deemed unacceptable, violations of the college's norms and regulations. The college also needs to have a plan for how it will proceed when students go beyond the rules and, for example, take over a building. Students' rights and responsibilities concerning freedom of expression should be clearly stated in college publications, along with the action the college will take if policies are violated. The worse scenario is to have to make up policies and procedures in the midst of a crisis. The role of campus security officers should be clearly defined as should be the circumstances under which the local police would be called onto the campus.

■ College demonstrations frequently attract media attention. Although few controls can be placed on the media, the college should decide who is going to officially represent it during times of crisis. All media inquiries should then be forwarded to the designated person. Colleges located in small towns may also have to work with concerned members of the local community. The community must understand what the college deems to be appropriate and inappropriate behavior on the part of demonstrating students and what action(s) the college will take if demonstrators engage in inappropriate conduct. The larger community may have to be educated about the special role of freedom of speech and academic freedom on a college campus and why it is such a crucial and protected part of learning communities.

There should be a designated representative of the college to the community. Parents are going to be concerned when demonstrations erupt on a college campus, and they often need to be educated in the same manner as the local community. Parents' most pressing concern, however, will be for the safety and welfare of their child, and the role of talking with concerned parents will usually fall to the office of student affairs and to the dean of students.

Controversy on a college campus is not something that always can or should be avoided. Too many administrators inevitably look upon controversy as a negative factor in the community. A liberal arts campus without a constant and healthy dose of controversy, however, is probably not doing a very good job of teaching the liberal arts. Students are learning to think for themselves, and administrators should not feel frustrated when they use these skills to examine critically the college and its policies and practices. College life provides students with great opportunities to apply what they have been learning, and apply it they will whether we want them to or not. Even in the midst of a controversy, the dean of students should view the disturbance as an educational opportunity, not a monumental headache.

To capitalize on the educational possibilities that accrue from controversy, the dean must be prepared in advance. He or she should have a cooperative arrangement with the student government association to work together when campus issues arise and to cosponsor open meetings, with a planned format, where the controversial issue can be discussed in the presence of concerned and knowledgeable people. The dean of students can be responsible for seeing that the appropriate administrative staff and faculty will participate, and the student government association can run the open forum and mediate the debate. By doing this, several goals can be accomplished: (a) Everyone on campus has the opportunity to receive information directly, rather than through rumor and second- or third-hand sources; (b) the issues can be discussed in relatively rational and controlled circumstances, rather than in front of an angry mob; (c) the issue can be discussed with a much more economical use of time, with a limited number of individual and group appointments; (d) consistent use of the open forums will help alleviate the suspicions about the motives of the administration that tend to run rampant on a college campus, and will demonstrate to students that the administration is willing to defend its actions in the light of the day; and (e) students can learn about the subtleties and complications inherent in what sometimes appear to be the simplest of decisions.

Campus Tragedies
As a dean of students, I have had to face many crises arising out of trag-

edies, with the most demanding resulting from the death of a student or students. On small college campuses, especially highly residential ones, the death of a peer can have devastating effects on other students. Aside from the single death resulting from illness, suicide, or accidents, multiple deaths resulting from van accidents and group activities are not uncommon. A college must be prepared in advance for such incidents, and, although it may seem somewhat gruesome, it is prudent to have written, unpublished procedures about how the college will handle these circumstances and who will be responsible for carrying them out. Some questions need to be considered well in advance: who will notify parents, and what to do if the parents are separated or divorced; who will notify college friends, roommates, and hallmates, and what support services will be offered to them; who will handle release of information to the press; and who will be responsible for memorial services. If these tragedies are not handled thoughtfully and competently by the college, students, families, and community members can be deeply hurt and offended.

The press, in particular, can be a problem in both student demonstrations and campus tragedy. Too often, they, like the students, are looking for a smoking gun where none exists. They sometimes invade privacy and interfere with the grieving process. Unfortunately, the more the institution tries to keep the press out of a situation, the more they may suspect that something is being covered up. Again, it is advisable to have one person on campus who deals directly with the press and have all other administrators and faculty refer calls from the press to that person. If the students do not wish to be interviewed, this must calmly but firmly be explained to the press. I was once involved with a group of students who had been on an outdoor recreation trip resulting in deaths and a horrifying experience for the surviving students. The students did not want to speak to the press individually, but we knew that information explaining the incident would have to be released. It was a particularly delicate situation, because there was the possibility that the college could be accused of negligence. When I spoke with the students, we decided to write a group narrative explaining the events, which everyone would then sign. It took hours of talking, writing, and rewriting to put together an explanation of the events that everyone felt was accurate. This group experience, however, was a powerful one which helped the students with their own grieving process, kept them from being isolated, and helped them to deal not only with the loss they had experienced but also with their guilt over their participation in the events which led to the deaths. It also gave the press the information they needed to provide the public with a first-hand account of the events.

The Well-Adjusted Majority

Given the many problems that a dean of students must confront, it may often be hard to keep in mind that most students on campus function quite well, taking advantage of the college's programs and generally thriving in the school's demanding and exciting atmosphere, without ever having direct contact with the student affairs staff. It can be so easy to get so caught up with the students who experience behavioral, psychological, academic, and social problems, that one can lose touch with the very students the student affairs program is primarily designed to serve. This can be a deadly trap.

College environments and student affairs programs should not be structured primarily to serve students experiencing emotional and behavioral problems. Instead, they should be structured to allow healthy, functioning students to take advantage of the college in order to develop fully their knowledge and skills. As a dean of students, I have found that I need to find the time to meet the "normal" students, who rarely if ever come through my office doors but benefit greatly from the environment the student affairs program has helped to create. Such students are exploiting the opportunities offered them and taking advantage of both the freedoms and the responsibilities of young adulthood. If a student affairs program is successful, most students may not recognize how important its efforts have been in providing a positive educational and social environment.

Even the best of programs must be constantly fine-tuned, taking into account the ever-changing interests and needs of the students, or it runs the risk of gradually losing its effectiveness. Constant monitoring, through discussions, written evaluations, and brainstorming sessions, must take place to assess how well students are responding to and taking advantage of the opportunities offered.

FACULTY

A degree of strain will always exist between the faculty and the student affairs program, due to the different roles each plays with students. This can and should be a healthy tension, however, and need not lead to polarization. In making generalizations about the faculty, I will try to avoid resorting to unfair stereotypes, but I make no promises that I will be completely successful. This section is not intended to be an analysis of faculty and faculty behavior, which I will leave to someone more qualified than I, but I will discuss how deans of students and their staffs can work successfully with the faculty for the benefit of the students.

It is imperative that the dean of students get to know the faculty, although even on a small campus he or she will not be able to get to know each faculty member personally. Still, on a relatively small campus it should be possible for the dean to know each faculty member by name and face. The dean does, in any event, have to learn the defining traits of the college's faculty and their academic orientation. What are the guiding beliefs and the distinguishing characteristics and sentiments of the faculty? What do they see as the mission of the college and the purposes of their teaching efforts? How do they view student life outside the classroom? What do they believe about student participation in curricular and other academic policy issues? What criteria are used for promotion and tenure decisions? The dean should also learn to understand the specific pressures that faculty are under — and are reacting to — at their particular institution.

In some ways, faculty are almost trained to be irascible. Their profession places high value upon critical analysis, the examination of premises, and the questioning of authority; independence of mind and a degree of cynicism are necessary for their success. Many faculty members could not avoid questioning the actions of the administration, including the dean of students, if they tried; to do so would be to go against everything they have been trained to do and to believe. Deans should try their best not to become overly defensive about faculty questions and criticism. These do not usually indicate personal dislike of the dean so much as a distrust of unexamined premises and unquestioned policies. Their training makes them very constructive critics, so an effective dean will be wise to seek out their advice and consultation. One need seldom worry about the willingness of faculty members to express their opinion.

Campuses vary a great deal in terms of how much the faculty is formally involved in student affairs programs, but on many of our small college campuses, the faculty have become very detached from student life outside the classroom. The professionalization of the student affairs function as well as the actions of the faculty have led to this situation, and it does little good for either group to blame the other. Rather, we need to seek out the faculty and demonstrate that we need them to be involved with and participate in student life.

I believe students should have a high level of involvement in governing student life programs, but colleges are educational not political bodies and cannot function as full democracies ruled by student majorities. Decisions must be in the best interests of the institution's educational mission, and, for this reason, the administration and particularly the faculty must have a significant role in deciding the policies and programs that determine what takes place in the residence halls, on the playing fields, within the Greek organizations, and in the other student activities that have a significant positive or negative influence on the quality of learning in the classroom. Members of the faculty should be concerned about the effect our programs have on the student's ability to be academically successful and should be involved in their creation.

Faculty members should be a part of all significant student-life related policy-making committees. It is the role of the dean of students to meet with faculty members and explain the importance of their involvement, describe the student affairs philosophy, discuss general concerns, and solicit their active involvement in the committees. If a faculty committee does not exist, the dean of students should take the initiative to establish an advisory committee of faculty, meeting about once a month, that can be called upon when special circumstances warrant. All involved should recognize, however, that this is not a policy committee but an informal group from whom the dean seeks advice.

The dean of students should become involved in all orientation programs for new faculty, which will give him or her the opportunity to discuss the institution's student affairs philosophy, to explain how the office can work with and assist faculty, to demonstrate how it complements and supports the primary academic mission, and to answer any questions that the new faculty member may have. This process also provides the dean with the opportunity to meet all new faculty members face-to-face. The dean of students' staff can also publish a small handbook for faculty members, explaining to them the services offered by student affairs and the ways that student affairs staff can effectively work with faculty members for the good of the student.

It is essential for the student affairs office to explain to faculty members what information the office can and cannot share with them, most importantly in relation to counseling and academic support services. Faculty members often, understandably, feel that the flow of information about students only goes one way. They tell the academic support office and counseling center everything they know about a student, and are told little, if anything, in return. A faculty member who knows a student well and cares deeply about that student will be frustrated when not given information by the student affairs office, so it is important that faculty members understand the importance and the justification for our stance on confidentiality. If not handled well, such situations can alienate sympathetic and supportive faculty from the student affairs office. Faculty members who recognize that students are having difficulty and refer them to student affairs for help are invaluable, and everything possible must be done to preserve their trust in the student affairs office.

It is especially important for the dean of students and the director of academic support services to be members of the college committee for academic policies and standards, particularly the committee that makes decisions on the academic probation, suspension, and dismissal of students. They can often be very helpful to the student and to the committee by providing information about extenuating circumstances that may affect student performance, such as a death in the family or financial or personal problems, so the committee can make more informed decisions that will positively influence student performance. Explaining and discussing the committee action with the students and their parents often falls upon the dean, and this task can be accomplished more effectively if the dean has participated in the committee decisions. This committee also allows the dean an opportunity to demonstrate to the faculty his or her commitment to the academic standards of the college.

The dean of students must also establish a good, cooperative working relationship with the dean of the faculty or provost so that he or she understands and supports student affairs programs. By meeting regularly with the dean of the faculty, the two can coordinate programs, keep one another informed on campus issues and concerns, and discuss ways to mutually support each other's efforts to achieve institutional goals. The dean of the faculty's support of student affairs can greatly enhance the dean of students' effectiveness and can demonstrate to the faculty the college's commitment to having academic and student life programs which complement each other.

Students will often bring complaints about the faculty to the dean of students or to the student affairs staff, particularly when they involve claims of unfair treatment in the classroom or in grading or of sexual harassment. This is an area fraught with potential problems. Most faculty members do not see the dean as having any authority over their actions, and they often resent any intrusion into their activities. It is important that the institution have policies and procedures that can be used when charges are made and that the procedures are carefully followed. It is best to work closely with the dean of the faculty, keeping him or her fully informed and trying not to step into his or her area of authority. Sexual harassment charges are especially difficult; whether or not they are found to be true, such charges can damage a faculty member's career. On the other hand, sexual harassment by a faculty member can be devastating to a student, and students need protection from such behavior. Institutions are now required by law to have sexual harassment policies and procedures, but establishing policies and procedures and using them effectively are two different things.

As the dean of students, I have found it essential to be involved in establishing sexual harassment policies and procedures to ensure they adequately protect students' rights and do not discourage students from filing complaints. I walk a fine line in this area: on the one hand, I do not assume responsibility for actively seeking out improper behavior on the part of the faculty; on the other hand, I do not ignore student complaints or persistent rumors about improper faculty behavior. Students subject to harassment by faculty members, staff, or peers must be protected by the institution, and it is often the dean of students' role to do so. The dean of students, however, should not act alone and should immediately involve the dean of the faculty and any other individuals called for in the college's harassment policies. If charges do come to my attention, I have both a legal and a moral duty to protect other members of the community and to see that there is an honest attempt to investigate the allegations.

The faculty should be involved in student life outside the classroom, and there are still discussions on small college campuses about the "good old days" when faculty members were highly involved in student life and student organizations, even living in the residence halls. Accompanying these reflections are often discussions of ways to reestablish these old patterns. This line of thought seems especially attractive to college presidents, but, given the great changes that have occurred — dual career families, longer living distances from campus, the part-time status of many faculty members — it would be impossible for the faculty to once again take on the role now assumed by the student affairs office. It may be possible, however, to have some faculty members live on campus and play a greater role in student life, as has been successfully accomplished at Stanford University for several years. This requires separate living units for the faculty and their families, adjacent to or very near the residence halls. We know that the faculty have a powerful effect upon students and anything the college can do to try to increase informal interaction between faculty and students is a positive move.

Other steps, short of having faculty members live on campus, can successfully increase faculty interaction with students. Most of today's faculty members would never think of simply wandering around the residence halls on their own initiative, but many respond very positively to being invited to residence hall functions. One successful program at Grinnell College made funds available to our resident advisers to bring faculty members onto the floors for evening study breaks with students. These were intentionally informal so the faculty members did not feel as if they had to perform; rather, they shared themselves with the students, often not even discussing their own specialty. Anything we in student affairs can do to increase the exposure of faculty to students outside of the classroom is a positive step, and residence hall staff are in a particularly good position to help facilitate this.

A small, private, liberal arts college is as good as its faculty. A faculty that truly cares about its students and is highly involved with them provides the key to educational excellence, and the dean of students should do everything possible to encourage and enhance the quality of student-faculty interaction, particularly that which occurs out of the classroom and is based on common intellectual interests. The dean can help faculty members become involved with students by promoting and supporting student-faculty cooperative research projects, student housing arrangements built around an academic project, language houses, and a variety of other activities that naturally bring students and faculty together around shared intellectual interests.

A dean will find that many faculty members at their own discretion become counselors and advisers to students with personal problems. One of the common mistakes made by deans is to try to capitalize on this phenomenon, to make counseling a formal part of the faculty's job description. Faculty members resent this expectation, do not see it as a legitimate part of their professional role, and will refrain from counseling students once it is formally demanded of them. It is most productive, therefore, to encourage those faculty members who willingly and effectively fulfill this role.

Student affairs administrators too often minimize the centrality and importance of the faculty and view faculty members as enemies rather than as colleagues with whom they are engaged in a common quest. This attitude seems to stem from a belief among student affairs staff that they are viewed as second class citizens in their institutions, that their role in it is minimized by the faculty and not adequately recognized. Deans must emphasize to their staff that the faculty is the core of the institution and that student affairs plays a supportive role to the central educational mission of the college. This is not to suggest that the student affairs office does not have an important, indeed crucial, function of which staff members can take great pride, but it does require acknowledgment of the central role of the faculty and the importance of constantly seeking constructive ways to work with faculty members.

The most important role that a dean of students can play in relation to the faculty is to gain its support and approval for the student affairs program and demonstrate that the program helps students to be academically successful. If the faculty believes in the student affairs program's commitment to student academic success, in its effectiveness and in the competence of the people in student affairs positions, the faculty will refer students to them for help and will seek out their advice.

PARENTS

The role of parents as a constituency group poses an interesting dilemma for a dean of students. Often they are paying all or most of the cost of education for their children, and, even if they are not, they are usually making a substantial economic sacrifice to send their child to a private college. Students will often turn to them first for advice and support, and they are often the first to offer constructive help. In other cases, however, they provide little or no financial support to the student, are the last source to which a student will turn for support and advice, and have a negative affect on a student when they do become involved.

A dean of students needs a consistent policy on how and when the student affairs office involves parents, and parents need to know what that policy is and the rationale for it. The institution as a whole also must have a consistent policy concerning release of information to parents, stating specifically the information it will not release without the student's permission. If a college does not have these policies in place and does not stick closely to them, it will be open to conflicts with parents and students, possibly involving lawyers, since many of these issues are covered in the Family Educational Rights and Privacy Act (FERPA).

Some institutions share almost all information with parents, while others share almost no information with them. Neither of these extreme approaches seems to work very effectively. The institution that shares all student information with parents not only runs the risk of having students withhold information from the college, but this practice also may violate FERPA rules. Often, students who want and need help will not seek it out if they believe their parents will learn about their problems. Institutions that share no information with parents, on the other hand, automatically cut off a potentially valuable resource for helping students and may alienate parents from the college.

In addition to the federal limits imposed by FERPA, many states have passed their own legislation affecting the distribution of educational records. Thus it is necessary that a dean of students obtain good current legal advice concerning statutory limitations before releasing information to parents. Private colleges often have more leeway to exercise judgment than do public colleges, but legal advice should still be sought to define exactly what limitations exist. After the legal ramifications have been detailed, institutional policies consistent with the overall college mission and student affairs philosophy can be developed. For example, if my recommendation that students be treated as adults and helped to assume responsibility for their own lives is accepted, there are significant implications for the relationship between the student affairs office and parents. Does treating students as adults mean that a dean never speaks to parents or shares information with them about their children without the students' permission? What if the students have not acted as adults or accepted the responsibilities that go along with status as an adult? It would be nice if there were a single correct answer to these issues, but they are among the countless gray areas that demand that judgment be exercised by the college and its dean. Most important is to work within a clearly defined framework that has been fully explained to both students and parents.

One approach to this dilemma which gives an appropriate message is to let students and their parents decide what information is to be released rather than having the college make this decision for them. A form can be sent to all new students and their parents, along with an accompanying letter explaining that decisions concerning parental access to information about student academic progress are best made by the student and his or her parents. The form allows the students and parents to choose between options ranging from parents receiving no information to parents having full access to the information and would be signed by both students and their parents. Careful handling of this potentially volatile issue is very important: parents who may be paying between $20,000 to $30,000 per year to send their child to college will often react quite negatively when refused information concerning the student's progress toward the degree. Even with such an agreement, however, it will be impossible to cover every situation; some judgment calls will have to made and the dean should be prepared to present a statement of the factors that were taken into consideration in making the decision.

Because absolute consistency can never be achieved, even I, who am very committed to a philosophy of treating students as adults, must back away from carrying this philosophy to its logical conclusion. There are times, usually involving threats to life or health, when the college must intervene directly in a student's life. Even in these cases, however, the involvement of parents is not a given. For example, although I generally believe that parents should be involved when their child has attempted suicide — an act that indicates that a student has given up responsibility for his or her own life — there are also times when mental health professionals will advise that the involvement of the parent will be detrimental to the student's recovery. Often, moreover, information about the student's health cannot be legally released to parents without a signed release from the student. At a small college, the dean of students will ultimately have to decide whether the parents should be notified and will have to be ready to defend the decision should difficulties arise. Aside from the legal restrictions, there are no set rules that can be applied in making these judgments. A dean has, however, a primary responsibility to the student and this must be honestly made clear to parents at the time of enrollment.

Deans of students also must decide whether to encourage parental involvement in the institution through parent associations. Serious thought should be given to this issue, and if it is decided to form an association, clear goals and purposes must be established at the beginning. Even with a clear mission statement, parents' associations can take on a life and direction of their own which may be quite different from the one that the institution and its administrators initially envisioned. Once parents come together in an association, ticklish political problems can arise if members start moving in directions that go against the goals of the institution and so have to be reined in. Parent associations are often formed for the wrong reasons, i.e., to raise funds for programs not included in the institutional budget. Most parents are already paying their fair share to the institution in the form of payments for tuition, books, and room and board, and the primary function of parental associations should not be to assume an even greater part of the burden of running the institution.

Parents, like their sons and daughters, have provided me with some of the best moments of my professional life, as well as some of the worst. Some parents refuse to see a child who has attempted suicide and refuse to even acknowledge the fact that the attempt took place. Others are wonderfully supportive people who helped their child get through a harrowing experience. It is a fact of life that there will always be parents who disagree with a dean's actions and that these parents will often be the most vocal. Because such parents tend to go immediately to the president, the trustees, and anyone else who will listen to their opinion about the dean's incompetence, it is a good idea to keep the president informed when a parent is unhappy. In any event, the best way to avoid problems is to be honest with parents about the policies of the student affairs program and of the college and then to apply those policies in a consistent manner.

The role of dean at small, private, liberal arts colleges has changed greatly in its level of complexity, its scope of authority, and in the nature of the expectations held. Given the context within which the dean works and the constituents he or she serves, it is also important to understand the unique challenges faced in the areas of the institution that the dean oversees. The supervision of those areas and their respective programs and services represents a significant portion of the dean's responsibilities.

Part II:
SERVICES AND PROGRAMS

The range of services supervised by the dean of students at small colleges varies from one campus to another. The supervision of these different services and their staff takes a major portion of the dean's time. This section discusses several services whose supervisory challenges demand detailed discussion: residence life, conflict resolution systems, student activities and organizations, career services, multicultural affairs, counseling services, health service, academic support services, campus security, food service, orientation, financial aid, and registrar. Each of these services demands significant direct student contact on a daily basis and each is important to the reputation of the student affairs program. I will also discuss the hiring, training, and supervision of residence life staff.

RESIDENCE HALLS

Most small, private, liberal arts colleges are primarily residential. The resources, energy, and staff of the student affairs programs are centered on the residence hall experience. A successful residence hall program can do more than any other student service to enhance a student's education, increase retention, involve the student with peers and the institution, and help the student develop mature social skills. On the other hand, poorly run residence hall programs can detract from the student's ability to succeed academically, increase attrition, isolate the student from peers and the institution, and thwart the development of mature social skills. Merely providing residences is not enough; there must also be a strong support program that students themselves see as beneficial. The final test of a good residential program is whether the students would choose to stay in it if they had a choice.

Based upon my professional experience, several components must be in place in order for a residence hall program to be successful:

■ There must be a commitment and a belief by everyone, including the faculty, that residence life is an important component for supporting student academic success.

■ There should be carefully designed physical facilities to provide students with comfort, security, living options, opportunities for interaction, and the possibility of privacy.

■ If possible, no living unit should house over 100 students. Most students on a small college campus prefer to live in units of 25-75 students.

■ No designated residence halls or floor should be assigned exclusively to first-year students, who should be integrated among upperclass students.

■ New student assignments should be made in a way that tries to assure roommate compatibility.

■ An ample number of single rooms should be provided, giving upperclass students an option for increased privacy while providing many alternate living options, including doubles, two-room doubles, triples, three- and four-room triples, co-ops, suites, special interest houses and floors.

■ A governance system within the halls should promote the involvement of the students and provide them with a significant role in controlling the residence halls.

■ There should be a variety of living options for students, including coed and single-sex halls or floors, or both.

■ Professional student affairs staff should live in residence, with an ideal ratio of professional staff to students of 1:150, but no greater than 1:200.

■ Student staff members should live on each residence hall floor. A ratio of student staff to students of 1:15 is ideal, but the ratio should be no greater than 1:25. The exact ratio will also be a function of the physical structure of the residence hall and the financial resources available to support a residence life staff.

■ The primary role of the professional and student staff should be a supportive one: to help the residents resolve problems and to create social, educational, and recreational programs, rather than to be proctors, rule enforcers, and providers of such programs.

■ There must be an excellent food service.

■ There should be a self-sustained ethos which encourages students to care about each other.

■ There must be a strong commitment to designing environments and programs that support student academic success.

Students are young adults and should be treated as such, even if some are not yet ready to accept the responsibilities of adulthood. In my experience, fewer than five percent of residential students cause nearly all of problems, leaving colleges with two choices: to create a system aimed at controlling the five percent, thereby restricting the freedoms and responsibilities of all the students, or to create a system aimed at giving the 95 percent the responsibilities and freedoms which will allow them to grow, to learn, and to develop values and social skills. It is, of course, better to have the five percent abuse the system and to deal with them in the best way possible than to stifle ability of the 95 percent to thrive and flourish in a system which shows them the respect they, as responsible adults, deserve. To put it simply, a college eventually reaps what it sows; if the system sows distrust of students, it will reap students who cannot be trusted.

If not done well, such an approach risks the establishment of residence halls where students accept freedom but not responsibility, or where a small minority of immature students hold the rest captive. This type of program cannot be implemented without a system that requires — and sometimes even forces — student involvement or without a strong professional and student staff who believe in and are committed to the program's success.

Students in such a program learn how to govern themselves, stand up for their own rights, and resolve their own problems. This will not always work perfectly, and it will sometimes be criticized by parents, faculty, students, and other administrators. The dean of students must believe strongly in this system, be willing to spend hours implementing and refining it, and be prepared to defend it to the end of his or her days. When the system works, students learn how to assume control of their lives and their living situations, how to effectively make compromises and resolve problems with peers, and how to strike a balance between the desire to protect their own individual freedom and the necessity of giving up some freedom for the good of the community. Teaching these lessons becomes an integral component of a liberal arts education. As it becomes the students' own program, it will enter into the college's hallowed tradition, and will be defended to the death. I know that I have succeeded when a program is no longer mine but the students', when it becomes so much a part of college life that the students would not allow it to be dismantled.

Professional Staff Living in Residence
To achieve excellence, it is crucial that professional *resident directors*, who, ideally, should have graduate training in student affairs, counseling, social work, or a related field, live within a residence hall. The primary duties of a resident director are to supervise, train, and consult with the student staff; to provide counseling and referral to residents; to work with the students to design and implement educational, social, recreational, and cultural programs; to serve as an adviser to the governance process; to handle emergencies and student crises; and to work closely with the students in creating a caring community. If possible, the resident director should *not* be a proctor for residence hall students, directly enforce college regulations regarding student behavior, or govern the residence halls. This may not be possible in all institutions, but it will be difficult for the resident director to simultaneously hold out a helping hand and an enforcement club to the students.

At both Grinnell and Reed Colleges, I have also had the resident directors work part time outside the residence halls in areas such as career services, academic support services, housing office, multicultural affairs, student activities, outdoor recreation, and educational programming. Resident directors will only stay in live-in positions for one to three years, and they will find advancement in the profession easier if they have experience in other areas of student affairs. By offering a wider experience, it will be possible to recruit good professionals as resident directors. Moreover, resident directors literally take their offices back to the residence halls, thereby making those offices and the services they provide more accessible to students.

The selection, training, and supervision of resident directors is a crucial factor contributing to the success of a residential program. The people who fill these positions must be able to relate comfortably with students, have a very real commitment to them and their welfare, display excellent judgment, have good counseling skills and knowledge of the developmental patterns of young people, and be able to present a model for good community citizenship. In general, resident directors provide a 24-hour adult presence in the halls and can immediately respond to all students' needs for help, advice, and consultation.

Residence hall staff should, at the very least, be as diverse as the student body. Although all staff members should be committed to helping students from under-represented groups, these students need advisers within the residence halls to whom they can easily relate, and who understand the special challenges they face.

Establishing a resident director program is, in many ways, providing a postgraduate student affairs training program. It takes a great deal of time to properly supervise and train staff at this level, and the task can be both tremendously frustrating and very rewarding. At least 60 to 70 percent of the dean's time is spent on efforts directly related to the residence hall program, and with on-call duty and night work this is greatly increased — it seems as if nearly all serious student problems take place during the night or on weekends. It is, however, extremely important to let live-in staff know that the dean is always available when they need advice or when problems arise that they cannot handle themselves.

Student Staff

A good *student resident adviser* staff is another essential ingredient for a successful residence hall program. In a good system, resident adviser positions will be sought after, not because they are well paid — in fact, at Grinnell College the resident adviser position was a volunteer one — but because the position is seen as an honor. An excellent program, even more than good compensation, will attract qualified students, so the quality of the applicants provides a barometer of the health of the residence hall program. Being a resident adviser is very difficult but highly rewarding; these students live on the same floor as the students for whom they are responsible, and although the role is demanding it also offers great opportunities for positively affecting the lives of fellow students.

Too many programs are not as successful as they could be because the primary responsibility for proctoring students' behavior and enforcing college regulations is given to student hall staff. This is an incredible burden to place upon someone who is a peer of the residents and who lives with them; because student staff members come to be seen as the enemy, they are often the last persons students will seek out for help and advice. The student staff's primary job should be problem-solving and community development, not rule enforcement. Their presence is necessary so that the students will be able to solve their own problems, to create a positive living and learning environment, and to assume the responsibilities of self-governance. The resident advisers must act as models of involved and responsible community living.

This does not imply that resident advisers should be passive in the face of vandalism or the violation of the rights of students. Rather, they should be the catalyst that gets students to stand up against the inappropriate behavior of their peers and helps them to protect their individual and collective rights. Their role is not to protect students from the reality of residence hall life and solve problems for them, but to teach and to help students resolve their own problems. If they carry out this role successfully, they will not become the enemy, wasting their energies in catch-me-if-you-can cat-and-mouse games, but will be seen as caring and involved friends to whom students can comfortably go for help to resolve difficulties and to find solutions to problems.

A good living environment cannot be forced upon students by the college. If it is to exist, the students must become actively involved in its creation. When the student staff takes on a helping, problem-solving, creative role, the program begins to attract students who do not simply want a job or a position of authority, but those who care about their fellow students and want to help them.

Student staff members must be very carefully selected, trained, and supervised. Helping students resolve their own problems and govern themselves requires more sophisticated skills than merely being able to enforce rules and monitor behavior. The training must concentrate on having knowledge and skills in the areas of individual and group behavior, conflict resolution, mediation, and leadership. It is crucial that resident advisers receive constant support and consultation from the professional residence hall staff.

Student staff selection normally takes place in the spring, and staff members begin their jobs in the fall of the next academic year. A carefully designed selection process guarantees not only that the very best people are selected but that the process is viewed as fair by the residents. Minimally, a candidate should provide recommendations from the student's resident director and from students on the floor where he or she is presently living, and be interviewed alone or as part of a group. The interviewing process should also be used to inform the student about the position for which he or she is applying. Students presently on the staff should be involved in the selection process.

Student staff should be provided with a very thorough job description and a clear list of performance expectations at the beginning of training, so they know what is expected of them and how they will be held responsible for carrying out their duties. In a program where the primary roles of student staff is to be a friend, an organizer of activities, a person who can recognize serious problems and refer them to the appropriate help, and a good mediator, careful selection is essential. These roles are not simple, especially when one considers that the student staff member is living on the same floor as those for whom he or she is responsible.

It is usually quite difficult to have an extensive training program in the spring after the new student staff has been selected. Selection tends to be a lengthy process, and by the time it is completed, the end-of-the-semester papers and finals are looming. Spring can be, however, a good time to have the staff members begin to get to know each other, to make plans for how they are going to work with each other next year, and to develop a team concept. One of the best ways to accomplish this is by having a two-day overnight retreat at an off-campus location. Going off campus is important to avoid distractions and to help participants concentrate on the tasks at hand. This period of time is used primarily for a series of enjoyable team and community building activities that help staff members to get to know each other and begin to develop working relationships.

Extensive training of student staff usually takes place in the fall of the year, prior to the other students returning to campus, and should be at least a week in length. Student staff members need a great deal of specific information about the college so they can be an information and referral source for students on their floor. The workshops can concentrate on preparing for participation in new student orientation, planning activities for the first few weeks of school, learning problem-solving and mediation skills, learning how to work with crisis and emergency situations, and developing an effective team that can help and support each other and the students in the halls. Some programs fail because they try to give all the required information to students orally during the workshops. The student affairs staff should prepare a very thorough student staff handbook that is mailed out to be read during the summer. The handbook should be organized so that the information is easy to find and should contain information about the college, referral sources, policies, deadlines, telephone numbers, and other information pertinent to the student staff job.

Based upon need and interest, workshops on specific topics such as AIDS, suicide prevention, eating disorders, multiculturalism, and leadership and organizational skills should be planned by the student affairs staff for the entire school year. Having non-residence hall staff, such as career services, counseling center, health center, multicultural affairs, international student affairs, and student activities involved in both these ongoing workshops and the fall workshops can have a positive effect. The training of the professional resident director and the student residence hall staff can be a process that brings the entire student affairs staff together and reinforces the concept of an integrated student affairs program. At some colleges it is possible to set up credit-bearing classes to teach and train the student staff. When this is possible, it can also be an effective way of recruiting student staff.

Resident directors must make themselves easily available to the student staff for consultation and be a part of their on-going training programs. The resident directors should consult with the associate dean or dean of students as necessary and offer on-going training and supervision of their own. A high level of commitment — time, energy, involvement, and concern — is required from the dean of students down to the student staff. To gain the desired outcomes, this group has to be well-coordinated with clearly understood goals.

If it is at all possible, the dean of students should not be directly responsible for the residence program and the supervision of the resident directors and the student staff. There is not enough time in the day for the dean to supervise these programs adequately. The residential program should be supervised by either the director of housing or, ideally, an associate dean of students who does not also have the day-to-day responsibility for the administration of the housing program, i.e., room changes, damages, and repairs. The person who fills this position should understand and believe in the college's residence hall philosophy and have several years' experience in residential programs. He or she will be the right hand of the dean of students, sharing the responsibility for late night and weekend emergencies, being available to the residence staff for consultation, and helping to relieve the dean from the otherwise impossible task of total responsibility for the residential program.

Coed Residence Halls

Another issue that arises in relation to residence hall programs is whether they should be coed and, if so, to what extent. All of my experience at small, private, liberal arts colleges leads me to be a strong advocate of coed halls, especially halls which are coed by alternating rooms. I have already expressed my strong dislike for residence halls that house only new students. I also recommend that new students be given the option of living in halls that are coed by alternating room. I do not advocate, however, that all halls be coed by alternating rooms, unless all students wish this option. If the institution requires its students to live in residence, it is obligated to offer both single-sex and different types of coed housing. No students should feel they cannot attend an institution because they are opposed to living in a coed system.

Grinnell College has had coed-by-alternating-room housing for over 20 years, and the experience has been overwhelmingly positive. Students who have lived in this situation tend to do better, both academically and socially, than those who do not. There are far fewer problems with vandalism, noise, and disrespect for the rights of fellow students in the coed-by-alternating-room halls. This type of housing tends to provide more pleasant places to live, with less sexism and healthier relationships, offering an environment that allows students an opportunity to get to know each other informally as friends, rather than being forced into a dating situation as the only means of developing relationships. Sexual stereotypes tend to break down quickly in a coed-by-alternating-room living situation. In fact, once this living situation is an option on campus, other living options, such as coed by floor and wing, do not even seem like coed living; they often come to be called single-sex by floor and wing. Although the experience at some institutions regarding coed-by-alternating-room residence halls has not been positive, I believe the problems may result more from the way the programs have been structured and staffed than from the concept itself. Coed-by-alternating-room residence halls, like any other system, can be problematic if not carefully planned, well staffed, and grounded in a strong ethic of caring for and respecting the rights of others.

Freshmen Residence Halls

To my knowledge, very little research has been done on the relative benefits of halls with only first-year students as opposed to halls with a mix of classes. Pascarella and Terenzini (1991), in their comprehensive review of the literature in *How College Affects Students*, only mention one study on the topic done by Whiteley (1982), which suggests that self-esteem may be bolstered by living in an all-freshmen residence hall. This boost in self-esteem, however, may come with a loss of the challenge to thought and action provided by upperclass students. At both Grinnell College and Reed Colleges, I have found that upperclass students provide a positive influence on new students. They are a ready source of information about the classes, majors, faculty, and how to get things done within the institution. They are often much more willing to challenge new students who breach community standards and violate the rights of others, and they can help new students become more readily involved in the college. Many new students get a bit carried away with their newfound freedoms, and often upperclass students can help to temper their high spirits.

Director of Housing

The director of housing holds a crucial but difficult position on a residential campus, one that needs strong supervision and support. The director of housing is responsible for the operational rather than the programmatic aspects of the residence halls. People in student affairs generally view themselves as helpful people, liked and appreciated by students, but they may find it difficult to say the word *no*. By definition, however, the housing director often has to say no to students. There are only so many living spaces on the campus, and even when the director would do anything to give a student who really has problems a room change or a single room, there simply may not be any available, or they may have to be given to another student who has even greater need.

The director also has to enforce housing regulations consistently and uniformly, even when they do not make a lot of sense for the particular circumstance of an individual student. The director of housing in a small college, more than any other student affairs administrator, is constantly caught between two conflicting student demands: (a) "This is a small college which claims to treat people individually, so why can't you make an exception to your stupid rules for me? My situation is different" and (b) "You have to be fair, treat me equally, and give to me whatever you have given to another student."

The daily pressures on a director of housing are tremendous, and a dean should be aware of this and lend support. One way to help is to assign to directors of housing some responsibilities outside the housing area, where they will have the opportunity to interact with students in a helping function. They might be assigned to work part time in the office of academic support, where they would help students having difficulties, or work with a student organization or committee that wants and needs help. The important thing is that the assignment provides housing directors with the opportunity to work in a role where students see them serving in a supportive and helpful capacity.

Students are understandably very sensitive to housing decisions, policies, and issues, and they will appeal many decisions and policies of the housing office to the dean of students — everything from housing assignments to fines for damages. Because of this, the dean needs to have a very thorough understanding of the housing program and a good, close working relationship with the director of housing. The housing director and the dean of students must work hand-in-glove with each other and agree on housing policies and enforcement procedures. The director of housing needs a substantial amount of support from the dean, or the tenuous authority he or she has will be severely diminished in the students' eyes. The dean of students who routinely overturns the decisions of the housing director had better be prepared to do the housing director's job because students will almost certainly learn to appeal all negative decisions to the dean.

Student housing is so important to a good college student life program that I advise anyone who eventually wants to become a dean of students to spend some time working directly in the housing office, ideally as both a resident director and as director of housing. Many would-be deans avoid holding the director of housing position, but this is a serious mistake. Most small college student affairs programs are built upon the residence halls, and a dean should be thoroughly familiar with every aspect of student housing. There is no better way to gain this knowledge than to be a director of housing. It may not be the most appealing position in student affairs, and it certainly is not the easiest, but it is a position where a wealth of knowledge about the most basic function of student affairs can be learned.

Creating and maintaining a good residence hall program is the greatest challenge a dean of students will face at a small, residential, liberal arts college. It is also the program with the greatest potential to truly enhance the college student's educational experience. The residence halls offer a unique opportunity to influence students' personal growth and development significantly and to assist in their academic success. Outside of, perhaps, a military barracks, there is no other place where a person will live in such a close environment with so many different people. Friendships will be formed which will last a lifetime, and lessons about human behavior can be gained that can rarely be obtained in any other environment. If a dean is forced to cut corners, the residence halls are the last place to do so. Every dollar, every staff position, and every moment of time given to the residence halls will be paid back tenfold.

CONFLICT RESOLUTION SYSTEMS

An excellent residence hall program also requires a clearly defined but flexible conflict resolution system. The system must be flexible enough to fit the problem and the individual(s) involved, rather than force the problem and the student(s) to fit the system, a problem-solving rather than a judicial system. The process must be fair, legal, and protective of the rights of all students involved in the dispute. It is a program which emphasizes mediation and one-to-one problem solving over adversarial judicial hearings. The attempt is to resolve difficulties at the lowest possible level, in an informal setting, with the students directly involved in deciding upon the best resolution. If a resolution cannot be reached through this informal process, however, a more formal judicial process must be in place to hear the case.

The informal resolution process is preferred for two reasons: (a) it requires an attempt on the part of the students involved to resolve, with help and support, their own problems and to talk with and learn from each other and (b) many students will hesitate or fail to use the judicial process because, once they initiate a formal hearing, control of the situation will be out of their hands. Like all citizens, students wish to have their rights protected but they do not want to be responsible for punishing another student too harshly. Offering control over the consequences is crucial to gaining student involvement in the problem-solving process.

Initial attempts at resolution of problems can take place by having the student staff member or the resident director meet with the students and attempt to mediate the situation. Students should also have the option of having the mediation take place with a more neutral party who is not directly involved. Grinnell College did this through a group called the Office of Community Rights, which offered a mediation team composed of one student adviser and one resident director who did not live in the hall of the students involved and did not directly know them. Mediation was always non-binding, and both parties to the dispute had to agree to a resolution before it was sanctioned. The College Judicial Council could also refuse to take a case and refer it first to the Office of Community Rights for mediation if it felt this was appropriate. Reed College has an Honor Principle, with very few written rules and regulations. The Honor Council has very similar duties to those of the Office of Community Rights, but the Honor Council is made up of an equal number of students, faculty, and staff.

In this conflict resolution system, the judicial council is always the last resort, except in very serious violations of student rights or college regulations such as assault, serious vandalism, or theft, or in cases like sexual harassment where face-to-face mediation may not be deemed appropriate. The goal is to resolve as many problems as possible outside of a judicial hearing, although it is extremely important to have the judicial system in place, with clearly understood procedures that offer due process. A judicial council should have a student majority, but also at least one faculty member and one administrator with student affairs background. The dean of students or his or her designated representative should be allowed to attend the hearings as an observer. The dean of students' office will usually have to deal directly with the student, the student's parents, and possibly even the student's legal counsel, a function much more effectively carried out if they have first-hand knowledge of what transpired in the hearing. There must also be an appeals board, composed of faculty, students and staff; all recommendations of the judicial board and appeals board go the president of the college, who makes a final decision.

Even at this level, the title "hearing board" is preferred to "judicial council," and the aim of the procedures is fact finding rather than adversarial. It is primarily the obligation of the hearing board to conduct the hearing and actively seek to ascertain the facts, rather than follow the judicial model, which leaves this burden upon the plaintiff and the defendant. Students may have an adviser from the college community to help them prepare their case but legal counsel should not be allowed to attend the hearings unless mandated by state law, and the defendant and the plaintiff should be required to speak for themselves. All of this should be in the written policy of the college. Either party to the case should have the right to request a hearing that is open only to those directly involved in the case, to avoid the carnival-like atmosphere which can result in open student hearings. To assure that students are adequately prepared for the hearing process, trained advisers should be available for students who cannot find one on their own. At Grinnell College, a student could use one of the mediating teams from the Office of Community Rights for this purpose. Whatever system is designed, however, the two most important things to keep in mind are that the system should do everything possible to encourage student use and guarantee fairness to all parties involved.

Student problem-solving and judicial systems must be especially sensitive to problems and incidents stemming from issues of gender, race, and sexual orientation; both individual and intergroup conflict have, unfortunately, become more common on our campuses. Too often students who feel victimized due to their status also feel that the established conflict resolution systems do not meet their needs, and they must have assistance and support if their rights are going to be protected adequately. In such instances, trained advisers who are trusted by the students can be of tremendous assistance. The conflict resolution system especially must be viewed as open and accessible to such students. Advisers who can support and assist them in utilizing the system can go a long way toward accomplishing this end.

The most important components of a good conflict resolution system are that it (a) be accessible, (b) offers alternative means to resolve conflicts, (c) does not, except in extreme circumstances, take the control of the process out of the students' hands, and (d) is fair to all parties involved. Another very important component is training. Mediation groups need very specific training that should be offered either by a staff member who has been trained in mediation or an outside mediation service. The judicial board also must have training prior to hearing cases, ideally including hands-on case studies which give them realistic experience with the types of problems they will face. A part of this training also can be a session(s) with legal counsel so they are fully informed as to their legal obligations under the college's particular judicial system.

STUDENT ACTIVITIES AND
STUDENT ORGANIZATIONS

The student activities office plays a very important role on campus, particularly if the college is located in a small community in a rural area. Even in an urban setting, however, the office plays a crucial role if the college wishes to make itself the center for students' social, cultural, and recreational lives. Rural colleges bring groups of bright, energetic people together in an isolated environment. Many of them have come from urban areas where entertainment and multicultural opportunities were taken for granted. The students who do come from rural towns look upon college providing an environment in which they will have social and cultural opportunities that did not exist in their small communities. An excellent social, recreational, entertainment, and multicultural program can provide students with enhanced satisfaction with the college, and help the college retain students. It is sad to see students leave a college where they are getting an excellent education because they feel lonely, isolated, and bored.

The best student activity programs allow students to be closely involved in their design and implementation and gain the participation of many students and student groups from across the campus, rather than of a few overworked students. Such student activity programs also encourage and promote a great variety of student organizations that appeal to a large number of interests. The primary task of the director of student activities is to encourage, solicit, and maintain student interest and involvement.

Student organizations present a real challenge to the student affairs program because each generation of students and student organizations may be tempted to waste energy and effort reinventing the wheel. Those who question this should look at the activity calender of almost any small college, which is typically nearly empty during the first two months of the fall semester and then jammed during the last two months of the spring semester. Too many student organizations take the entire first semester to get organized and figure out what they wish to do. Lack of continuity in participants, knowledge, and organizational structure is the worst enemy of student organizations. Unfortunately, every year many organizations start all over again from scratch.

A good student affairs program will provide strong support services to student organizations to help them avoid the problems mentioned above. A dean of students should try to do the following:

■ Provide a full-time staff member whose primary responsibility is working with student organizations.

■ Make it clear to the rest of the student affairs staff that they are all expected to work with this staff member and with student organizations.

■ Create office space for student organizations which is located adjacent to, or near, the student affairs offices. Each student organization does not need a separate office; the organizations can share offices, telephones, duplicating equipment, computers, meeting rooms, and work rooms. The director of student activities should be located in the same area.

■ Encourage the student government to adequately fund and support student organizations.

■ Give flexible hours to the staff member working with student organizations, so he or she can be in the office during some evenings and weekends, when students are most active.

■ Provide organizational and leadership workshops for student organizations. Combine these with workshops provided for the residential staff, to save resources and to give staff an opportunity to get to know the students in the organizations.

■ Help connect student organizations with the residence halls and floors, recognizing that residences are made to order for encouraging group activities.

■ Try to get to know the student organization leaders and let them know that the student affairs office recognizes their importance and wishes to work with them. Meet with these leaders at least once a semester for a discussion of their needs and concerns.

The professional staff member who works with student organizations is crucial to a good program. If the college cannot fund a full-time position, consider using a professional resident director part time in this position. The purpose of this position is not to run the student programs, but to help, assist, and advise the students in running their own programs. The first task is to help the organizations structure themselves to overcome problems with continuity. Filing systems, libraries, resource people, telephone numbers, funding sources, position descriptions, recruitment procedures, budgeting procedures, organization manuals and constitutions, and space reservation procedures all need to be established and maintained. The organizations must be structured so there is carry-over in leadership positions from the spring to the fall and in planning for the fall training and training of new student organization leaders in the spring.

The director should write and keep updated a student organization manual that describes the college budgeting procedures and all policies concerning printing, advertising, space utilization, telephone, mail, speaker contracting, and publications. Student organization leaders can also be brought back to campus for workshops prior to the beginning of school in the fall and given time to do the last-minute organizational tasks needed, so their activities can start immediately upon the opening of the college year.

Student committees or clubs can be established to run film programs, speakers programs, and concerts, but the best student activity programs do not simply leave it to these committees or clubs to provide all of the programming on the campus. The multicultural student organization, the international student organization, religious organizations, the gay/lesbian/bisexual student organization, the women's group, environmental organizations, and the residence halls should, ideally, all be involved in bringing films, speakers, and entertainers to the campus. On an exciting and involved campus, the films and concert committees will only select and book about a third of the films and concerts. A major part of the committee's job will be working with the other groups, helping them organize activities. If a tradition can be established of having all of these groups actively involved in putting on programs for the entire campus, it will ensure a rich diversity of programming.

Another crucial aspect of the best small college activities programs is that they become all-campus events. Concerts, films, dances, speakers, and parties are events open to everyone on the campus. In the most outstanding college social environments, private parties, dances, and social events are almost non-existent; some small private colleges even have regulations which forbid closed activities or organizations.

Major dance concerts, speakers, and films, in particular, are seen as gatherings of the entire student community, a time when everyone comes together for a shared experience. The collective use of student funds also allows for better quality bands, films, and speakers to be brought to the campus than can be obtained when funds are shared among a number of smaller social groups. Some prerequisites for creating this type of community social environment that should not be overlooked are: (a) major indoor concerts, speakers, and parties require a facility which can hold at least 60 percent of the student body, and (b) such all-campus social environments are most commonly found at colleges that do not have active and successful Greek organizations that sponsor closed events.

Social, multicultural, and recreational programs should all be under the office of student activities. A good program benefits from having an active outdoor recreation group which sponsors activities readily available in the geographical location, such as biking, running, spelunking, sailing, canoeing, horseback riding, climbing, camping, and hiking, and, if possible, offers group student activities away from the college over college vacation periods. A strong intramural program is necessary, one which stresses both traditional team sports and other activities such as table tennis, pool, frisbee, and chess which allow less athletically inclined students to become involved.

Some student organizations will require direct involvement by the dean of students' office and often of the dean of students. The first of these is the student government association. The best student government is a strong one, so the dean of students must use every opportunity available to strengthen and support this organization. The dean should, if possible, serve as an immediate adviser to the student government association and meet with its officers at least once a week. The dean should want the members of the student government association to be well informed about what is going on at the college and to see themselves as partners with the student affairs office in attempting to improve student life. This may be easier said than done, however, since student government association officers often run on an anti-administration platform and begin their term of office with negative attitudes toward the dean of students. If the student affairs program is a very good one, part of this problem will already be solved, since students will not tend to see student affairs as part of the administration. Generally, however, I have found that most students are not opposed to working with the administration, as long as they are dealt with openly, honestly, and as adults.

The student affairs office should never get involved in student politics and, in particular, student government elections. Although it may sometimes be difficult to refrain from getting involved, especially when students with clearly negative attitudes are candidates, deans of students must accept and work with whomever the students decide to elect, without attempting to interfere in the process.

Deans of students at a predominantly white college also often need to work directly with the multicultural student group. Many small colleges never had significant numbers of students of color until the middle to late 1960s when they made the first organized recruitment efforts toward African Americans. At that time, the Rockefeller Foundation, as part of its commitment to the well-being of humankind and equal educational opportunity, provided minority student grants and scholarships, and many small liberal arts colleges used these to encourage the enrollment of minority students. Due to lack of experience with students of color, however, many did very little to cultivate an environment which was inclusive or to establish programs to meet special needs. In their attempt to be heard and have their concerns addressed, students of color often used tactics of confrontation and demonstration.

One of the most frustrating aspects of working with multicultural organizations is that it sometimes seems that no matter what I do, or how hard I work on their behalf, it remains difficult to win the trust of their members. Part of this is because members of any minority group, no matter what a college does or does not do, are going to have feelings of isolation and alienation which will, in turn, cause feelings of distrust and anger. This is part of human nature and we, as administrators, need to recognize this and not become discouraged because many of our students of color are unhappy with us or the college. We still should continue to work on the behalf of these students.

Commitment and continuity of effort are the two most essential and crucial ingredients required when working with multicultural student groups. As with the student government association, the best multicultural student organization is a strong one. The dean of students should play an active role in strengthening and supporting this organization and not leave sole responsibility for it to the director of multicultural affairs. A major difference in working with these organizations is that it may be necessary to reach out and demonstrate commitment more often than with others.

As a white male, I realize I am walking on shaky ground when writing about women's organizations. Over the years I have spoken to many deans, male and female, about women's organizations on the college campus. From these conversations and my own observations, I have concluded that many women's organizations on the small liberal arts campuses have had problems with continuity and effectiveness. Often this is due to their desire to use a leaderless organizational model. If they choose this model, they may need assistance in helping to make their organization effective and consistent. As with multicultural organizations, women's organizations have often been born out of controversy and have a tradition of confrontation with college administrations. A strong and active women's organization, however, can and should be a real asset to the college and to its students. It can help sensitize students and the college to the special needs and concerns of women and help to bring needed educational programs to the campus. The student affairs office must work with women's organizations to help them find an effective organizational model with which their members feel comfortable and which will ensure a continuity of purpose and effectiveness. The dean can also encourage these organizations to make alliances with other student organizations and, in particular, with the student government association from which they can receive valuable support and financial assistance.

Gay/lesbian/bisexual student organizations also have often been formed as a reaction to discrimination and have often taken a confrontational stance in relation to the college administration. Many institutions still do not have an official policy against discrimination based upon sexual orientation. No other student group has seemed to challenge college policies against discrimination to a greater extent in recent years than have these groups. Acknowledging them and their organizations has raised concerns and questions very similar to those which arose when colleges were deciding whether to admit their first black students, or when all-male colleges were considering admitting their first female students. Will we become a primarily a gay/lesbian/bisexual college? Will it ruin our fund-raising and alumni support? Will the publicity hurt our admissions effort? Can we survive the controversy of recognizing gays/lesbians/bisexuals as a group that we protect from campus discrimination?

These fears seem largely groundless. Any negative repercussions will most likely be limited to a small number of trustees or alumni. A potential donor may not make a gift, but this risk is incurred with almost any action a college takes. Should we, for example, not admit African American students because a donor will withdraw support? I think not. Colleges need to be truly non-discriminatory in their admission processes and also in regard to student programs and organizations.

Gay/lesbian/bisexual students need and want understanding and help from our colleges. If they are to achieve a legitimate status on campus, the dean of students' office must take on a leadership role. On some campuses, this will not be an enviable task; however, it is one that must be accepted if we are to provide the welcoming environment that will allow members of these groups to take full advantage of their educational opportunities.

Fraternities and Sororities
I apologize in advance for being so negative about fraternities and sororities on the small, private, liberal arts campus. I was a member of a fraternity and I understand their attraction, but I have severe reservations about the appropriateness of their presence at the small college, particularly ones which are primarily residential. For far too long, student affairs administrators have refused to openly address the existence of fraternities and sororities on our campuses. Deans are understandably reluctant to be open about their concerns on their own campuses. Greek organizations, while often providing a positive experience for many of their members, too often cause problems and have even been an embarrassment to our institutions.

For many years, I met on a yearly basis with the deans of students from the Associated Colleges of the Midwest (ACM) consortium and the Great Lakes College Association (GLCA) consortium. These two consortia represent a large number of some of the very best small liberal arts colleges in the Midwest, many of which have recognized Greek organizations. These meetings were roundtable discussions where the deans shared problems and concerns as well as solutions and programs. Each year there were lengthy, rarely (if ever) complimentary, discussions about Greek organizations and fraternities in particular. It was readily apparent in these discussions that most of our problems with alcohol, drugs, vandalism, and harassment involved fraternal organizations.

Greek systems may have a legitimate place at larger institutions, where there is a greater need for smaller, structured social groupings. In the small college residential environment, however, they can work against the community ethic of the residence halls and undermine the attempt to create a campus community. By their very nature, they are an exclusive rather than inclusive group. Small liberal arts colleges should decide whether to allow any groups that do not have open membership. This should be a considered decision made with full awareness of what type of community best supports a liberal arts education.

Regardless of my personal preferences, many colleges have Greek organizations on their campuses and, in most cases, they are there to stay. For this reason, fraternities and sororities must receive a great deal of attention from the dean of students. A staff member in the student affairs office must be given the responsibility, as well as the time, to work closely with Greek organizations, and this person will require a great deal of support and supervision.

Colleges with Greek systems must develop clear standards for the members of these organizations and make these standards consistent with those set for other student organizations. For example, it is not advisable to set up separate conflict resolution and judicial systems for Greek organizations. As much as is possible, these organizations need to function within the same system as do all other students and student organizations. If the Greek organizations are housed within the residence halls, for example, they should be under the same system and live with the same regulations as do the other students in the hall. Personally, I think Greek organizations should not be housed in a residence hall because it often places the other students living in the hall in the untenable position of being outsiders in sections of their own residences.

To help establish a positive Greek system, and to demonstrate the concern and interest that the college has in the activities of fraternities and sororities, the dean of students should meet at least once a month with the leaders of the Greek organizations. The very positive contributions Greek organizations can make to the community, for example, in the form of leadership training and community service projects, should be stressed. Students from Greek organizations are often disproportionately involved in student activities and campus organizations. On campuses where they have their own houses and food services, they provide excellent opportunities for gaining experience in management, governance, and business. A good Greek adviser can be very useful in helping members acquire the management skills needed to run good housing and food services. This can also be a way to involve the director of student housing and the director of food service in a consultant and training role with these students. Due to the loyalty of students to the organizations, they can also offer effective academic assistance to members who are having difficulties. Greek organizations should be asked to set specific goals in regard to how they are going to have a positive influence on their members and make positive contributions to the college community. These goals should then be reviewed with the Greek adviser or the dean of students, or both.

Student activities and organizations are the backbone of good extracurricular programs at small colleges. They can make the campus come alive and provide an opportunity for students with widely varying interests and skills to become involved in the institution. They can help to bring ethnic, cultural, religious, and social diversity to the programs of the college. Student activities is, however, an area of student affairs which is often understaffed and neglected. Too often students are left on their own to organize, fund, and provide these services for their fellow students. Students need help and support in this area if they are going to gain the maximum possible benefit from their involvement.

CAREER SERVICES

On many small, private, liberal arts college campuses the career services office is the least-understood and least-supported office in student affairs. In my experience, it has been especially neglected by the faculty, for whom it represents a careerism and vocationalism that is contrary to the values of a liberal arts education. The more prestigious the college, the more prevalent this faculty perception seems to be. For this reason, the career services staff needs to receive some very special attention from the dean of students.

More than any other student affairs office on campus, career services must know and understand the ethos of the faculty and the academic programs of the campus. The director has to be both diplomat and salesperson and must have a great deal of patience. The program and philosophy of the office must complement and respect the liberal arts. Many faculty members are becoming much more understanding of career services and its proper role on the liberal arts campus, but many still see the liberal arts solely in terms of learning for learning's sake and for them the very word "career" is a sign of an enemy within the camp.

Career services does have a legitimate and needed role on the small liberal arts campus, as long as its primary objective is not placement but teaching students to: (a) translate their liberal arts education to the job market, and (b) learn the life-long skill of finding their own jobs and careers. Good career services offices now spend much more time in teaching, advising, and counseling than they do in pure placement. Students need help in determining their career interests, writing résumés, acquiring interview skills, researching the job market, and learning how to make their liberal arts education work for them in the world.

The career services office is also the best place on campus to administer internship programs, student volunteer programs, and perhaps even the college's work study programs. When these programs are administered by the career services office, they can be structured into a true learning experience, one in which students can explore the potential of different careers and consciously seek to apply their liberal arts backgrounds. Successful internship and volunteer programs must be run by trained counselors who will work individually with students and the intern sponsors to assure a positive learning experience.

Most faculty members simply do not have the time, the training, or the interest to perform this time-consuming role on a consistent basis. Decentralized departmental internships too often end up being hit-or-miss affairs with little quality control and too little follow-up with the student intern and the sponsor. With these programs located in the career services office, it is natural for the counselor to help the student translate experience into a résumé, an analysis of educational strengths and weaknesses, and a plan for the future.

Proper staffing is always an issue for career services, and many such offices are understaffed and overworked. These offices can particularly benefit from a good professional resident director program that allows the resident directors to work part time outside the residence halls. Most graduate programs in higher education now offer programs in career services as part of their training, so many professional resident directors come to the college with both training and interest in this area. Using the resident directors as part-time career counselors also literally takes the office into residence halls. If the student affairs program does not have professional residence hall staff, the use of student workers and student interns also can offer much-needed assistance, as can the use of alumni volunteers.

The primary energy of the career services staff must initially be aimed at developing partnerships with the faculty. No career services program will be successful on the small liberal arts campus if it does not consistently receive referrals of students from the faculty. This requires that the director work closely with the academic departments and conduct basic research concerning each academic field and how its students can fit into to the job market. Another important task of the director is working with the alumni of the college and getting them involved in helping students find careers and jobs. Loyal alumni can be one of the greatest assets to students looking for advice, mentoring, and employment.

MULTICULTURAL AFFAIRS

The director of multicultural affairs position is one of the most difficult in higher education, and I still sometimes have doubts about whether the position is a feasible one. If there is such an office, deans of students must be aware of the unique pressures that are placed upon multicultural affairs directors and their offices and attempt to provide support and assistance.

One of the biggest obstacles that can develop for a director of multicultural affairs comes not from the students but from the faculty, staff, and the institution itself: the expectation that the director is the expert on all issues and problems affecting minorities and that he or she will be responsible for directly dealing with all issues and problems relating to students of color. Once a director of multicultural affairs has been hired, many people and offices come to believe that they do not have to deal directly with multicultural issues and problems but can — and should — refer them to this director. This is a tremendously unfair burden to put on one person, and it also works against establishing an institutional sensitivity to students of color that successfully helps them to feel a part of the college.

The director should be kept informed of situations involving students of color, and certainly can be consulted, but it is extremely important that other staff members and administrators work directly with minority students, just as they do with all students. The dean of students must actively define the role of the director of multicultural affairs to the faculty and staff and encourage them to interact directly with students of color and their issues, rather than simply referring them to the director.

The director of multicultural affairs is also often placed in difficult situations by students of color. On small college campuses, the director is often the only minority administrator or one of a small number of them. The students see the director as their advocate and have a sense of ownership about the position and the person filling it. This can lead to several problems: (a) students will take problems to the director which they should be taking directly to other faculty or staff; (b) they will expect the director to support and defend them, regardless of the circumstances; and (c) they will expect the director never to reveal negative information about students of color to anyone else, including the director's immediate supervisor. The director of multicultural affairs is thus often placed in an untenable situation by the very students he or she is hired to help. This problem is compounded if the director of multicultural affairs is a young administrator with very little experience.

Another danger that faces the director of multicultural affairs is professional compartmentalization. Most people of color come into the profession of student affairs with the same aspirations and goals as do their non-minority peers. They wish to eventually be promoted to positions such as associate dean or dean of student affairs and to make contributions to the entire college. Too often institutions restrict their work solely to multicultural concerns and do not offer them the broad experience in all areas of student affairs that they will need to be promoted and to be successful in their field. One way to help multicultural affairs directors with this problem is to structure the job so they are working outside of multicultural affairs on a part-time basis. Another is to encourage other staff and other student affairs offices to include them in their programs, not for multicultural issues, but rather in areas where they can use their general student affairs skills and expertise.

A strong multicultural affairs office can have very positive benefits for students and for the college. Students of color need special services and support to help them to overcome the natural feelings of alienation and isolation most will feel on a small, predominantly white campus. A multicultural affairs office can organize the campus to provide this support, and can help to make the students of color feel they are wanted, valuable, and contributing members of the campus. The director of multicultural affairs can be of great assistance to the institution in helping to educate faculty and staff about the special needs of students of color and in establishing more effective means of working with these students on a daily basis. A good multicultural program helps bring cultural and educational programs to the campus, not only for its students of color, but also to broaden the experience of the non-minority students. Students of color are becoming increasingly sophisticated in choosing colleges, and an active multicultural affairs program will be visible proof to prospective students and their families that the college is committed to the education of students of color.

The final means for evaluating a college's performance in this area should be linked to the retention and graduation rates of students of color. This cannot be the sole responsibility of the director of multicultural affairs or, for that matter, of the student affairs division. Retention and graduation rates are institutional obligations for which all constituent groups have significant responsibility.

Many members of any minority group on a college campus are going to experience feelings of alienation and isolation, and have a greater struggle in achieving academic and personal success than will be the case with most members of the non-minority population. On several predominantly white campuses, I have found students of color to have major dissatisfactions with the institution. If, then, the dean's major goal is to get these students to love the college, he or she will likely become frustrated and disheartened. A much more attainable goal, and one that will do more in the long term for students of color, is to make sure that the graduation rates of students of color are equal to or higher than those of our majority students. It may not be possible to make all students of color happy with the college, but they should all receive the assistance and support that will keep them in college and allow them to graduate.

Issues relating to multiculturalism have torn and are tearing apart many small colleges, in some cases leading to the Balkanization of campuses. Too often, even student groups are at odds with each other over scarce resources and staffing issues. We must find better ways both of making our campuses more multicultural and inclusive and of having students, faculty, and staff work together for common goals.

COUNSELING SERVICE

A good professional counseling program, with staff members who understand and work well with students, is an essential service on a college campus. It is also a service that is difficult and expensive to implement in the small college setting, leading to a number of problems common to many small college counseling centers:

■ There are often only one or two therapists, giving students little or no choice in terms of the gender or ethnicity of the therapist or of the therapeutic approach.

■ The confidentiality that is so important in this area may be hard to guarantee at the small college, where anonymity is very difficult to achieve. All students fear that information given to the counseling center will somehow end up on their official college record, and this fear is increased at small colleges, where everyone knows everyone else.

■ The responsibility of running a one- or two-person counseling office with on-call responsibilities is extremely stressful.

■ The costs of operating an adequately staffed center with excellent personnel for an eight-month academic year is very high and often involves an inefficient use of resources.

Counseling and health services, particularly for colleges located in small towns and cities, present an area where serious consideration should be given to establishing cooperative services with the local community. Such an arrangement can be beneficial for the college and the community: it can improve mental and physical health programs for both and, in particular, help to solve many of the problems, mentioned above, that are inherent in small college counseling centers.

Many communities in which colleges are located already have private, public, or private non-profit mental health facilities. If they do not, there is almost certainly a need for them, which could be met through a cooperative college and community effort. Several different models can be used to implement this program. I will give details of one such model.

College-Community Mental Health Clinic

A private, non-profit mental health center can be established which provides services to college students, faculty, and staff, individual members of the local community, the local hospital, county-supported mental health patients, local businesses, the public school system, and other public and private agencies that desire them. A board of directors representing the above groups as well as the local medical community is established. A director with a degree in either psychology or psychiatry is hired and reports directly to the board. The director is responsible for the overall operation of the center, including the recruiting, hiring, training, and supervising of professional and support staff. If the director is not a psychiatrist, a part-time contract must be arranged to provide psychiatric services and supervision. The center attempts to hire therapists (social workers and certified counselors) from diverse backgrounds who have a variety of training and experience.

The center is financed by contracting for services with agencies such as the college, the county, businesses, and the local school systems, using individual insurance premiums, individual payments, and state funding if available.

The college has several options in determining the level of service provided to its students and the method of payment to the mental health center. These options include:

■ The student is entitled to unlimited visits to the mental health center, with no direct cost. The college contracts with the mental health center to provide the services for either a single set amount or for an hourly amount for services actually performed. The college builds its costs into its tuition and fees, or both.

■ A set number of visits (four to ten) to the mental health center is established, for which there will be no direct cost to the student. Any visits above this number will be billed to the student on a sliding fee scale, or to the student's insurance carrier.

■ All students are required to carry a college insurance policy covering a predetermined first-dollar amount of mental health coverage, or submit proof of having their own policy with the same or better coverage. The mental health center collects all payments through insurance billings. The college could also elect to be self-insured and collect the insurance premiums from the student.

■ A set number of visits to the mental health center is established for which there is no direct charge to the student. The student is required to carry insurance, as in option three. The college pays the mental health center a predetermined overall fee. The mental health center collects the insurance and pays it back to the college.

As can be seen from the above, there are many different options to use in contracting for services with the mental health center and for financing the services. The goal is to establish a service which does not discourage a student from using it for financial reasons and yet still places reasonable limits on the college's financial and legal liability. In its initial stages, much publicity and information will have to be given to the students about this service. The student affairs office should be responsible for this educational program and the mental health professionals must be willing to spend time on the campus — in the student union, and in the residence halls — introducing themselves and the services they offer. Part of the contract with the mental health center should call for consultation services for the student affairs office and for educational programs for both students and student affairs staff to be provided by the mental health staff. Depending upon the location of the service, it may even be necessary to provide students with transportation.

The advantages to the college in having this type of arrangement are:

■ Usually the cost to the college will be significantly less to contract out these services than to provide them itself, particularly if the college already provides more than one therapist. If college cost estimates include salary, fringe benefits, offices, secretarial assistance, supervision, and professional development, the difference will be even greater.

■ Many students actually prefer an off-campus counseling center which is independent from the college, because they perceive it as being more confidential and objective than a college center.

■ A cooperative arrangement with the community allows for a larger number of therapists and counselors, with a choice of gender, race, ethnicity, or of different therapeutic approaches, and provides greater access to mental health services than can a college center.

■ The staffing of a mental health center allows for 24-hour, on-call services.

■ The student affairs staff is provided with a greater variety of professionals with whom to consult and from whom they can receive training.

■ The college's legal liability for the services provided is nonexistent or significantly lessened.

■ The college has an independent source for assessing severe behavioral and emotional problems of its students.

While dean of students at Grinnell College, I helped to establish such an arrangement, one which has now been in existence for more than 20 years. The service has been well accepted by the students, with approximately 10-13 percent of the student body using the services each year. The arrangement has also allowed for greatly expanded mental health services to the residents of the county and to the city of Grinnell, Iowa. I established a similar program during my one year at Western State College in Gunnison, Colorado. A counseling center, which was not highly utilized, had previously been on the Western State campus. I strongly recommend that small colleges seriously consider some variation of this model.

HEALTH SERVICE

Providing adequate health care to students is also a difficult proposition for small colleges, particularly those located in rural communities. The increasing cost of providing these medical services, and the shortage of good physicians and nurses who are willing to work solely with college-aged students, have compounded the problem. Small colleges have taken many different approaches to the delivery of health services: some have complete health centers with their own physician(s) and nurses, pharmacies, laboratories, and bed facilities; some have nurse practitioners or physician assistants; some have only nurses, who provide screening and treatment for minor illness; and some have elected to assume no responsibility for their students' health care.

What is the obligation of a small college for the health care of its students? I propose that it is to ensure: (a) that adequate health care is available to the students; (b) that the health care needs of the students do not overwhelm the health care services of the local community; and (c) that the students the college brings to the community have adequate resources or insurance to pay for health services. This does not imply that the college itself must provide comprehensive health services to its students. Just as with college counseling services, good health services are expensive and difficult to provide at the small college level and are ripe for cooperative efforts with the local community.

It is not reasonable in this day and age to duplicate health services in small or large communities if a joint effort could benefit both the college and the community. Deans of students must take the initiative to work closely with local physicians and hospitals to attempt to create cooperative efforts in providing health care. As with mental health care, there is no one model which can or should be applied to all situations. So many differences exist in the health care services of the communities in which colleges are located that the college will have to work with its medical community to establish a program that will efficiently and effectively meet its students' health care needs. There are several different designs possible for cooperative programs. The following are two examples:

■ Negotiate a contract with the local hospital and physicians to use the hospital emergency room as the college health center or to use another walk-in center which has nurses, nurse practitioners, physician assistants, and physicians who provide basic medical services. Hospital beds would be used for overnight care, with payment made by the student's insurance if there is a justifiable medical need for hospitalization. The contract would cover the costs not covered by insurance for students requiring overnight care, such as the need for a quiet place to rest, isolation due to communicable disease, or emotional stress. The cost to the college for the contract could be covered by a student health service fee.

■ Keep the college health center open during the day with nurses on duty to screen students and determine whether they need to be seen by a local physician. Nurses could also provide treatment and over-the-counter medication for minor illnesses such as sore throats and colds, and, with physician approval, provide some testing. Nurses would primarily run the program, but a physician, the medical director, would issue whatever medical orders the nurses needed to legally operate the center. The physician would not physically be on the premises. A contract would be negotiated with the hospital, similar to that mentioned above, for overnight care of students. All students requiring a physician's care would be referred to local doctors. Health fees would cover the health center costs; students and their parents would be responsible for physician costs. In some states, a nurse practitioner could be used rather than a physician.

In both of these cases, it may be necessary to provide transportation to the hospital or to physicians who are located at a distance from the college campus. This can often be done by using a college vehicle and student drivers. Both of these options would be feasible only if the local hospital routinely has more beds available than it has patients, which is the case in many instances. If not, it would be necessary to build a small, separate overnight unit for students who require overnight care but are not ill enough to be hospitalized.

Health education is also an extremely important component of college health services. The contract should provide for health education both on the individual patient level and in the forms of workshops and presentations on the college campus. Consultation services for the student affairs staff also should be part of the contracted services.

The primary point is that colleges and the towns in which they are located must be creative and cooperative, so they can devise an arrangement which does not needlessly duplicate scarce medical resources. In most instances, both the community and the college can benefit from such arrangements. Colleges must make certain that there is provision for adequate medical services for their students, but this does not mean that the college must meet this need by establishing its own separate medical delivery system. In urban areas, for example, a small college could align itself with a health maintenance organization (HMO), become a point of service provider for that organization, and have a student HMO policy to provide care beyond point of service.

Managed health care is here to stay, and it has made the delivery of both health and counseling services very complicated. If a college is going to maintain and run its own programs, it should consider combining health and counseling services into one unit supervised by a single director. For college students, health and emotional issues are often interrelated. I have had situations where a physician in the health center was prescribing one psychotropic drug to a student and the counseling center, without knowing what the health center was doing, was prescribing another drug to the same student. A holistic approach to helping students with health and emotional problems is necessary; this can best be achieved with a single health services program that offers both health and counseling services, has a single director, common charts, and where all staff consult regularly with each other about a student's treatment plan. The director's position in this arrangement is crucial. Not only must the director be able to provide direct services to the student, but he or she must be an excellent manager and have a real interest in national health care management issues.

The field of health care is undergoing rapid change and colleges can no longer afford to ignore the larger health world. Many colleges have provided health services without attempting to collect health insurance dollars to reimburse themselves for the expense. In all likelihood, colleges will be forced to align themselves with health care organizations in the near future. Health services are becoming increasingly complicated, and I urge all deans to pay serious attention to their programs so they can be prepared to take advantage of changed circumstances in this area.

ACADEMIC SUPPORT SERVICES

The primary function of a good academic support office at the liberal arts college is to provide advice, counseling, and help to students experiencing academic difficulties. Most students who are experiencing academic difficulties at small liberal arts colleges are also experiencing personal problems, and the academic support office must help these students overcome the personal and motivational problems that are impeding their academic success. Academic support services also provide faculty advisers with support and training.

The academic support office is a supportive service rather than an academic program and it should be a part of the student affairs program and supervised by the dean of students. If proper and coordinated help is to be given to the student, the director of academic support services must work closely and cooperatively with the counseling and residence hall staff.

Too often appropriate help is not given to students because the campus offices are not coordinated in their efforts. One office often does not know that a student is receiving help from others. For this reason, I also recommend that all academic support services such as reading, writing, and math labs be under the supervision of the director of academic support services, and that the staffs of these offices meet together regularly to coordinate their efforts on behalf of individual students. The director of academic support services can be located with the other student affairs offices and should be a member of the committee on academic standards. This is another office which can greatly benefit from having professional resident directors working within it on a part-time basis.

At most small liberal arts colleges the faculty have the primary role in the academic advising of students, particularly in regard to their progress through their academic program. It is essential that the academic support office works very closely with faculty advisers and has a role which is clearly defined not to conflict with or undermine that of the faculty adviser.

As mentioned above, students at selective colleges who are experiencing severe academic difficulties almost always also have some type of personal or motivational problem. This requires a good early warning system so that students who are having academic problems in more than one course are identified early in the semester, when help can be offered before it is too late for them to salvage their academic program. One approach I recommend is the required development of a progress plan for all students experiencing academic problems, in particular for all students placed on academic probation. The plan is structured so that it creates a working partnership among the student, the faculty adviser, and the academic support office. The written plan is a collaborative effort among these parties to decide what the student must do to get out of academic difficulty and what the college will do to assist the student in this endeavor.

Academic support services are crucial if we are to meet our responsibilities to our students. With the present state of our kindergarten through 12th grade systems, there is reason to believe that even higher demands will be placed upon this service in the future. An academic support program which is well coordinated with health and mental health services, faculty academic advising, and residence life can offer a valuable service to students and get them the assistance they need before it is too late in the semester to be effective.

CAMPUS SECURITY

At many small colleges, campus security does not report to the dean of students. Student affairs administrators who move from large universities to small colleges are often appalled by existing security programs. Some colleges located in rural areas do not even have what could accurately be called a security force. They have night watchmen whose primary responsibility is to monitor the mechanical systems and lock and unlock doors in the college buildings. These staff members have little or no security training and rely upon student affairs staff or the local police when problems arise. More and more small colleges, however, are establishing security offices as part of their risk management programs. Regardless of the level of security on the campus, there are some important things that must be done.

If at all possible, campus security should report directly to the dean of students. If not, there is a risk that the student affairs philosophy concerning the relationship between staff and students will be undermined by the security personnel. It does little good to have a student affairs philosophy that treats students as adults if campus security consistently treats them as if they were juvenile delinquents.

Regardless of the reporting structure, it is important that the dean meet several times a year with campus security officers and that the residence hall staff, including the director of housing, meet with them weekly. Campus security personnel often feel they are not appreciated, that the importance and difficulty of their role is not understood, and that they are given little support for decisions they often must make in the late hours of the night. The dean must consistently let them know that they are supported and considered an integral part of the student affairs team, and that the institution is concerned about their problems. The philosophy of student affairs and the means used for implementing it must be explained to them thoroughly, with specific examples given demonstrating how the philosophy should be applied in the type of situations security will handle. One way to win the loyalty and support of the security personnel is for the director of housing and other appropriate residence hall staff members to meet with security every Monday so that the student affairs office can be made aware of any problems that arose during the weekend and immediately take whatever follow-up action may be needed.

Another aspect of security is the campus security force, or lack of it. As mentioned previously, small colleges either tend to have trained campus security officers or have a campus security staff that consists of untrained night watchmen. Some small campuses located in rural settings really do not have a need for their own security force, particularly if local police will respond quickly to calls from the campus. If a campus does have its own security personnel, however, they must have proper training and excellent supervision and support. They must, at least, be equipped with two-way radios and, preferably, cellular telephones. They should always have immediate access to a supervisor who can help them in situations calling for judgment and to local law enforcement agencies.

Residence halls present special security challenges on the small college campus. Students cannot truly perform well if they do not feel their persons or possessions are secure. Security systems will vary from campus to campus, depending upon whether the particular setting is urban or rural and what kinds of problems the college has experienced. The primary problem in providing security is the conflict between the student's desire for easy access to the halls by the residents and their friends and the need to provide adequate security for the residents, their property, and the physical facilities. One apparently easy solution is simply to lock the halls and give the residents keys or cards to the external doors. Three problems, however, hinder this approach: (a) students often forget to carry or keep keys; (b) students who do not carry keys love to block open external doors; and (c) students who cannot get into a building will sometimes break windows.

Many colleges have been forced to staff a 24-hour security desk to let people in and out of the halls. This is a tremendous waste of resources that could be used for other purposes, but in some situations it may be the only practical solution. One problem with this is that many small colleges have small living units and thus a large number of halls, each of which would require separately staffed security desks.

Among the alternatives to security desks is to center security at the door to the individual student's room. Invest in very good, solid-core room doors, with the best locks money can buy. If keys are used rather than electronic key pads or cards, do not give out master keys to anyone but professional staff; require a stiff deposit of at least $50 for student room keys; immediately re-core any door when a key is lost; lock external doors in the evenings, but key external doors so each student's room key also opens the external doors of all the residence halls on the campus; and hold students responsible for any damages to or theft from the common areas of the residence halls. A similar approach differs only in that students' room keys will only open the external doors of their own residence hall. Security phones should be placed at external entrances, so if friends from another hall visit, they can simply phone the residents to ask them to open the door. New computerized card-key and key pad systems not only have the ability to offer greater security but also provide information about who entered a building and at what time. Although they are expensive and raise the questions of student privacy, they should nevertheless be considered.

One simple fact, however, needs to be faced: There is no such thing as a perfect security system. The only true security many institutions can offer students is excellent security at the door of their room, with a best effort to offer adequate security for the building. One cautionary note: never promise security to students and their parents which the college cannot deliver. Many students and their parents are becoming much more concerned about security issues than they have been in the past and are asking specific questions about it when they visit the campus. I try to make sure that both the admissions staff and my staff are being honest with them in describing the security systems. If a college is ever sued over a security issue, the first thing that will be asked in court is what security they promised to deliver. If the college did not deliver on its promises, it will have lost the case before it begins.

Again, I strongly recommend that campus security report to the dean of students. Over 90 percent of their contact will be with students, and it is essential that security personnel be part of the student affairs team and share their philosophy. It is also very important that a good working partnership be developed between the campus security officers and the residence hall staff; these work best when they are in close coordination with each other concerning all problems that arise in the residence halls.

FOOD SERVICE

There is probably no more thankless task on a college campus than running a food service. Not only does it have the impossible task of trying to please the individual palates of hundreds of students, it must also provide catering for functions run by highly critical faculty and staff members, presidents, and trustees. Directors of the food services have difficult jobs and also need the support and help of the dean of students. Easy targets for everyone on the campus, their turnover rate is often high.

There are almost as many contracting and reporting arrangements for food service directors as there are small colleges. Many colleges contract out their food service; many do not. Many colleges have the food service directors report to the business manager or vice president for administration; many do not. I am not attempting to build an empire for an already overloaded dean of students, but I believe that it is very important for food services to report to the dean of students. Food service provides a basic need to the students which is crucial to their satisfaction with residential life. The quality of the food is not the only important issue. Of equal importance is the environment and manner in which it is served and the efforts of the food service to carry out the overall student affairs philosophy. Students spend considerable time in the dining halls. They are not only places to eat but places to socialize, discuss issues that have been raised in the classroom, meet other people, and plan activities.

A good food service, working closely with the student affairs staff, can greatly enhance residential life and facilitate positive social interaction among students. Food and snacks are a social lubricant for students, and a good food service program should not end at the doors to the dining hall.

Food services can be involved in helping students have study breaks in the residence halls and floors; allowing for small groups of students to make special meals which they share together; providing the opportunity for groups of students to have outings, social events, meals and study breaks with faculty; and helping students get through finals week without ending up looking as if they have arisen from their deathbeds.

This can best be done if two things are in place: (a) the food service reports to the dean of students and is a part of the student affairs staff; and (b) the funds paid for the food service are not drained off to be used for other purposes. Many campuses look upon food services as a profit center, and too many campuses support non-board functions with student board funds. Neither presidential entertainment nor faculty and staff functions should be supported by the student board service, and the food service should not be used as a way to augment the general fund. It is simply not fair to the student who is paying for food service, often as a requirement of living in residence, to subsidize other functions. A creative food service program can do wonders for a residence hall program and can help to build a positive community. It is an opportunity which no good dean of students will forego.

ORIENTATION

The orientation of new students and their parents to the campus is another crucial student affairs function. Surveys I have conducted on the small, residential, liberal arts campuses at which I have worked indicate that new students have two primary concerns. First, they are concerned about their ability to meet the demands of the academic program. The more selective the college, the greater the concern. Second, they are concerned about how they will get along with their roommates and their hallmates. For many, it may be the first time they have shared a room with someone else and the first time they have lived in such close proximity to so many other people their age. Both of these concerns can lead to high anxiety levels during the first part of the school year.

In planning orientation, it is important to keep these major student concerns in mind and directly address them in the first few days. Programs should be designed to introduce new students to their faculty advisers and to both the formal curriculum and the informal academic expectations of the college.

The formal curricular program and its requirements are best explained by a combination of faculty and academic support staff. The informal academic expectations are best explained by a combination of students and the academic support staff. These meetings cannot be allowed to just happen; they require good planning, with clear goals based on prior research concerning the needs of incoming students. While the presentations should not be sugar-coated, they should also not create needless anxiety. A tone of caring and concern must be established, along with explanations of why many capable new students need academic assistance. Students must understand that the goal of the college is to assist its students in achieving academic success and that seeking out help is an acceptable and normal practice.

In the residence halls, the student staff plays an invaluable role in helping to orient new students to residence life. In fact, on campuses that are highly residential, it is often a good idea to give the office of residence life primary responsibility for coordinating and organizing orientation. Some structured time must be set aside to introduce students to the often unwritten norms and ethos of residential living and to have floor and roommates develop some common expectations concerning how they will live and relate to each other. At both Grinnell and Reed Colleges, for example, we created structured exercises for roommates that enabled them to discuss their personal backgrounds and habits, assisted them in making agreements about living arrangements within their room, and helped them to decide upon the means by which they would settle problems which might arise during the year. It is also a good idea to have the student staff hold a meeting on the floor, where students develop a kind of social contract, outlining how they will live with each other.

At the small, private, liberal arts college, many parents accompany their child to campus during orientation. The parents have a unique set of concerns and need information about the college and its services. Parents often have mixed emotions: on the one hand, they are happy and pleased that their child is attending college; on the other, they are sad to be separating from them and frightened of what might happen. Many times the fears are even greater for parents who have not themselves received a college education. Parents of students of color often have real concerns about bringing their child to a predominantly white institution. Many parents need information about the college and how it will or will not relate to them as parents. They also need reassurance that the college really cares about their child and wants him or her to succeed. Leaving a child at college can be a nerve-wracking and anxiety-producing experience for many parents, and it is a good idea to openly acknowledge this and offer to meet individually with parents who would like to do so.

The dean of students should put on a program during orientation specifically designed for parents that gives them an opportunity to hear from the dean and other critical student affairs staff. A short presentation by the dean, followed by questions and answers, is quite effective. In the presentation, the college's philosophy on student affairs should be described, along with some basic factual information about the college, and a consideration of what their son or daughter may experience over the next four years.

In describing the college's student affairs philosophy, it is important to let parents know what the college's goals are and how these goals affect the means for achieving them. For example, I talk directly to parents about our goal of helping students become responsible for their own lives and explain that, to us, this means treating students as adults and not assuming an *in loco parentis* role. It is also important to explain to parents some of the things that may or may not happen to their children while they are in college. In doing so I mention that (a) their sons and daughters will be intellectually and personally challenged and that this might bring on a degree of discomfort, lack of confidence, and confusion; (b) their sons or daughters might have some of the personal problems typically associated with the tremendous personal growth and development that occurs during the 17 to 21 age period and point out that if they do not experience such problems, it probably means they are not growing; (c) students might consider or take a leave of absence, but this rarely means they are going to drop out of college; (d) their child will change and that they might not approve of some of the changes; (e) parents should anticipate that the student might become a bit arrogant and overbearing about his or her new knowledge, values, and independence; (f) their son or daughter will not always think that the college is God's greatest gift to American youth; and (g) parents should not expect their children to understand how hard it is for them as parents to leave their child at the college.

It is crucial to explain clearly to parents how the college will and will not communicate directly with them about their children. It is advisable to include a clear explanation of FERPA and the limitations it places on a college's ability to reveal information to parents without student consent. It is essential to convey to them that, on the one hand, I want and need their assistance and support, while, on the other hand, how and why I will not, at times, be able to share with them all information concerning their child. This presentation should be upbeat and positive, but also should be realistic and not misleading.

FINANCIAL AID

The office of financial aid is one that has different reporting structures on various small college campuses. At many colleges, it reports to the dean of students, on others to the vice president and treasurer, and on some to the vice president for enrollment and director of admissions, or both. Regardless of the reporting structure, the dean of students must work closely with this extremely important student service. The financial aid office should not report to the office of admissions. While these two offices must, by necessity, work closely together, a separation and independence from each other helps the financial aid office to retain its service orientation toward students rather than having its primary emphasis be upon attracting students to the institution. Admissions officers are under tremendous pressure to deliver numbers of students, and its goals are not always compatible with the goal of delivering good financial aid services to the individual student.

A good director of financial aid is not always the easiest person to find. The heightened use of technology and increasingly complicated federal regulations require that a director have excellent technical and managerial skills. At the same time, it is important that this person also have good human relations and counseling skills. The financial aid office has a significant amount of direct personal contact with students and parents. The office works with highly confidential financial information and is often dealing with students and parents who are upset, angry, or confused. Many of the regulations governing the use of financial aid are complex and difficult to understand. A capable financial aid officer has to be good at technology, management, teaching, counseling, and human relations. If he or she lacks skills in any of these areas, problems will end up on the dean of students' desk, and many students and parents will be dissatisfied.

Another reason it is important for the financial aid office to work closely with the dean of students' office is to assist the dean's office in identifying students who are in distress and need assistance. Financial aid officers are often privy to a wealth of information concerning the problems students are having, particularly family problems. The sharing of this information with the dean of students has to be carefully considered so it does not violate parent or student confidentiality but, if done right, the financial aid office can provide another early warning system so that students with problems get needed assistance.

OTHER ADMINISTRATIVE OFFICES

The dean of students and the student affairs office will have working relationships with nearly every other administrative office on the campus. To be effective in delivering services to students, the dean and other members of the staff must establish effective ways of working with other offices. This is often easier said than done. Some key offices with which the dean works on a regular basis are admissions, the registrar, and the physical plant.

In the past, the office of admissions has not usually reported to the dean of students in most small colleges; rather, it has reported to either the provost or the vice president and treasurer. For this reason, I have not included it under the Services and Programs section. This reporting structure has been changing to some degree, as colleges have begun to use enrollment management models, but among small colleges it is not yet clear what enrollment management structure will predominate. Presently some schools are placing their dean or vice president for student affairs in charge of enrollment management; others have the dean of students reporting to the vice president for enrollment management. At still others, they have separate reporting functions to the president or provost.

Many years ago, it was not uncommon for the registrar functions to be part of student affairs; today, the registrar more commonly reports to the provost or to the vice president for enrollment management. The physical plant most often reports to the vice president and treasurer or to the business officer.

Admissions Office

The admissions office is something of an oddity in higher education. It is a marketing, sales, and public relations office in the midst of an institution that idealistically wishes such functions did not have to exist. Demographic realities and lower enrollments have softened this attitude in recent years, but at the more selective institutions, it still is part of the college's ethos.

The demands placed upon admissions offices today are enormous. In the face of declining applicant pools and higher tuition, they are asked to increase the size and quality of new student classes, recruit more women and students of color, find better athletes and musicians, and to do all this while awarding less financial aid. Unlike most other areas in higher education administration, the results and effectiveness of admissions is quantifiable and can be charted on a daily basis. The stress under which admissions officers are placed is tremendous, yet their efforts often are unappreciated by many at the college.

Deans of students need to be cognizant of and sympathetic to the pressures and demands placed upon admissions while at the same time being extremely concerned about how admissions is presenting the college to prospective students and about what type of students they are admitting. The admissions office recruits the students, but the student affairs staff will have to live with the students they recruit — and to live with the promises made to those students.

The admissions office can intentionally or unintentionally cause the dean of students' office many problems. It can make promises that cannot be fulfilled: "Sure, any new student who wants one can get a single room." "Don't be concerned about roommates. If you want a room change, you can easily get it." "Anyone who wants to live in a single-sex residence hall is able to do so." "Free tutors are available to students in all courses." They can ensure they will meet their admissions quota by going over it by 20 percent and cause severe overcrowding of new students at the most crucial time of their college career. Without giving any notice to student affairs, they can admit students who have just been in a psychiatric hospital for several months or who have just attempted suicide. They can admit students with learning disabilities without giving advance notification that accommodations will be needed. In short, it is possible for the admissions office to be responsible for consuming hours of your staff's time.

A dean of students can act to prevent some of these problems from developing. To begin, the dean should create a very positive working relationship with the director of admissions. Once this is accomplished, the student affairs staff can help to write and edit all brochures used by the admissions office that describe the philosophy and practice of student affairs at the college. Members of the student affairs staff should meet with all prospective students and their parents when they visit the campus and be an integral part of the recruitment program. There should also be an attempt to have the student affairs staff involved in the training of both new admissions staff and student hosts who accompany prospective students around campus. At Grinnell College, the student affairs office published and edited a new student handbook which was written by students and given to all prospective students. The student affairs office should communicate directly with all new students as soon as possible. If it can be done, it helps to have someone from the student affairs staff, trained by the dean, transfer to the admissions office and bring to it knowledge of student affairs and a student affairs perspective.

Ideally, student affairs and admissions should work closely together to achieve the twin goals of the admissions and retention of appropriate number and quality of students. For this reason, I am becoming increasingly convinced that admissions should become a part of the student affairs division, as it shares with it common goals and philosophies.

Registrar's Office
A close working relationship with this office is necessary, particularly if academic support services are a part of student affairs. At liberal arts colleges, students who are having academic difficulties are often also having personal ones, and the first indication that a student is experiencing problems occurs when there is a sharp decline in his or her academic work. The registrar and the office of academic support should work together to establish an early warning system in which, early in the semester, faculty members report students who are not attending classes, failing to hand in assignments, or are not passing the course. The office of academic support then needs to seek these students out actively and offer them assistance.

As I earlier recommended, the dean of students and the director of academic support services should be members of the academic standing committee which reviews the student's progress toward the degree and makes decisions regarding academic actions: warning, probation, suspension, and dismissal. In many small colleges, the registrar chairs this committee, which also has faculty representatives, usually from each division. Student affairs and the registrar must work together to create a balance between maintaining the academic standards of the college and considering mitigating circumstances that have contributed to a student's academic difficulties. Although often not an easy balance to achieve, success requires that both the registrar and the dean of students clearly understand and respect each other's roles.

Usually the registrar is instrumental in developing and proposing academic policies relating to standards of student progress toward the degree while the dean of students has the best first-hand information as to how these policies affect students. As anyone who has been an administrator for very long knows, regulations often have unintended secondary effects or do not work in practice as they were intended to in theory. When these unintended effects occur, the dean must work with the registrar and the academic standing committee to correct instituted policies. Student record-keeping issues also have to be coordinated between the two offices, particularly in areas relating to FERPA. The registrar and student affairs offices are usually the primary keepers of student records and they must strive for consistency in their practices with students, parents, faculty, and alumni.

Establishing good relationships with the registrar's office is not always a simple matter. Two of the primary roles of registrars are to enforce academic rules and regulations and to maintain sensitive institutional records. They have to say no to students quite often and enforce unpopular deadlines. They have a very different role than do many who work in student affairs. Both offices must, however, understand and appreciate each other's role and work together effectively, although this may require some effort on the part of the dean of students.

A student affairs office provides a model to other offices in their attempts to provide effective services to students and to earn students' respect. This will at times require that a member of the student affairs staff act as a mediator — and sometimes an advocate — for students in their dealings with other offices, a role that requires diplomacy if the other offices are not to be alienated. One of the best ways of accomplishing this is by serving as an example of positive, effective behavior.

Many administrative offices, such as financial aid and the registrar, have to enforce and live with regulations which they did not create and sometimes do not even believe in, causing them at times to be defensive and abrupt with students who challenge them concerning these regulations.

Many staff members have neither the training nor experience to work with angry and upset students. They are not insensitive and uncaring people, but they are ill-prepared for confrontation. Where such situations occur, it is often useful for a student affairs staff member to accompany the student to an appointment and, in doing so, to demonstrate effective interaction with angry and upset students. The student affairs staff can be helpful outside the context of a specific problem by organizing workshops for administrative staff members on how to diffuse anger and distrust when working with students. If the college wishes to create a caring environment for its students, all involved must learn to interact with them in a positive manner.

Physical Plant

A good relationship with the director of the physical plant can be a godsend to the dean of students, and a dean who can befriend a physical plant director can offer him or her needed advice and consultation. Do everything possible to establish a good relationship with the physical plant director and to facilitate a good relationship between the physical plant director and the director of housing. Again, it is important to take the time to thoroughly explain to the physical plant director the philosophy and goals of the student affairs program in general, and specifically to apply them to the residence hall program. The director must understand not only *what* student affairs is doing but *why* it is being done in the manner it is. Especially in the residence halls, the support of the physical plant is needed in order for the programs to be successful.

One of the first campaigns of a new dean of students should be to win over the physical plant staff. Meet with them, make up special brochures explaining what the student affairs office is doing and why, periodically set up sessions where they are asked for their ideas and advice, and try to create a working partnership with them. It is a major coup to get the physical plant director, the housekeepers, plumbers, janitors, carpenters, and electricians to understand and support the housing program, and one that will save the dean, the residence hall staff, and the students hours of time and energy.

Physical plant directors and staffs are a great learning resource. They know about the structural and mechanical strengths and weaknesses of the buildings, fire safety systems, furnishings, and lighting. They have taught me how to read blueprints, as well as providing a wealth of information

me how to read blueprints, as well as providing a wealth of information which has helped me to be more effective in lobbying for residence hall improvement funds. In return, the dean can help the director by providing insight into the unique traditions and ways of small, liberal arts campuses. A dean of students who has a good relationship with the physical plant is a fortunate dean indeed.

Providing leadership for the broad spectrum of programs and services supervised by the dean present unique challenges and opportunities. Yet, as noted earlier, neither the dean nor the dean's staff operates in a vacuum. Communication and collaboration with other areas and constituents within and outside of the campus have significant impact on the work of the dean and the areas he or she supervises.

Part III:
ORGANIZATIONAL
ISSUES

This section is about a series of organizational issues which are of importance to the dean of students. These include: the reporting relationships of the dean, the working relationship with the president and the president's cabinet, interaction with the board of trustees, the role of college committees, supervision of college renovation and building projects, and the hiring, supervision and evaluation of student affairs staff.

INSTITUTIONAL HIERARCHY

Most commonly, the dean will report to the president, the provost, the vice president for administration, the dean of the faculty, or to someone in a position that combines some of these roles. The reporting relationship, depending upon both the title and the personality of the supervisor, can have a tremendous effect upon the dean's ability to run a good program. It is usually preferable to report to the president of the college because the dean is able to represent the student affairs program directly, rather than through intermediary, to the ultimate decision-maker of the college. This relationship also assures that the needs of the student affairs program will not be presented to the president by someone who has a conflict of interest or who does not fully understand the program.

It is not uncommon, however, to have the dean of students report to the chief academic officer of the college: the provost, vice president for academic affairs, or the dean of the faculty. This reporting structure is usually instituted for the commendable purpose of trying to assure that the student life functions of the college are compatible with and supportive of the primary academic functions of the college. The problem with this reporting structure is twofold: (a) The chief academic officer usually has no student affairs training or experience; and (b) in a world of limited resources, the academic officer will often be faced with the decision of setting priorities that take into account the needs of student affairs and of the faculty.

The academic officer's limited training and experience in student affairs, coupled with academic demands, too often results in the dean of students being shortchanged both in terms of insightful supervision and of resources given to the student affairs program. When it comes to basic financial issues, for example, like whether to add student affairs positions or faculty positions, the chief academic officer's training, expertise, and understanding of the institution's needs will be weighted heavily to faculty concerns. Deans of students are placed in an untenable position: if they wish to go to the mat for resources that can meet what they see as the essential needs of the student affairs program, they may have to go over the head of their supervisor to the president. This can cause a severe strain, not only on deans of students' relationships with their supervisor, but on the president's relationship with the chief academic officer.

The reporting relationship cannot be breached very often without severely weakening the organization, which may cause the president to support the chief academic officer, even when he or she believes the dean of students is correct. One effective way to attempt to overcome this potential problem is through the regular use of written reports, with the request in advance that they be shared with the president; if the supervisor agrees, the reports can be copied to the president when written.

I always prepare a written end-of-the-year report that outlines the previous year's goals, accomplishments, and problems, as well as the next year's goals, intended means of accomplishment of those goals, and the resources that will be needed for successful implementation. Interim reports, once or twice a semester, can be written to update this report and to discuss new problems and needs that have risen during the year. Yearly budget requests can also be used not only to present budgetary needs but also to fully explain the student affairs program. If completely informed about the student affairs program, the president may support it even when the chief academic officer does not, thereby eliminating the need for the dean of students to appeal to the president over the supervisor's head.

Usually deans of students have little to say about their reporting relationship. The structure is in place when the position is accepted, and it is not negotiable. This does not condemn deans to failure if they do not report to the president. Many deans have been able to run good programs while reporting to the chief academic officer and have benefited in many ways from this structure. It does mean, however, that the dean is going to have to be much more persuasive, demonstrate excellent political skills, and spend a lot of time and energy teaching the supervisor about student affairs in general as well as keeping him or her constantly informed of what is currently going on in the program.

The personality of the dean's supervisor is always important, but even more so when the dean reports to the chief academic officer, due to the inherent potential conflicts of interest. The faculty can always put pressure upon the chief academic officer and, indeed, make his or her life miserable, with little fear of negative consequences; the dean cannot and should not do this. The faculty can and will use political pressure; the dean can only use reason and persuasion.

Every coin has two sides, however. On small, private, liberal arts college campuses, the faculty often have a much greater influence than they recognize. Faculty support of the student affairs program is, therefore, a crucial element in its ability to be successful and to gain the resources needed to accomplish its mission. A good chief academic officer who supports the dean of students in dealing with the faculty can be an invaluable ally in garnering faculty acceptance and approval of the student affairs program. When considering taking a position where the dean of students reports to the chief academic officer, consider whether the chief academic officer is seeking a strong advocate for student life programs, expects the dean to fight for the program's needs, and is willing to accept conflicts with the dean that do not harm their professional relationship.

Another less common relationship for the dean of students is to report to the vice president of the administration, who is usually in charge of all primary administrative offices and the administrative budgets and is sometimes the chief budgetary officer for the college. One advantage of reporting to this officer is that he or she is not responsible for the academic program; therefore, a conflict of interest is not as likely to exist as it is with the chief academic officer. In all likelihood, this administrator will be more seasoned and will have worked his or her way up through the ranks, and will thus have had more experience supervising non-academic offices. If this vice president is the chief budgetary officer, however, he or she will still be subject to some of the same pressures outlined above. A disadvantage is the probable lack of direct influence with the faculty, compared to that of the chief academic officer. Usually the vice president will not be as effective as the academic dean in helping garner faculty support for student affairs programs.

Even when deans do not report to the president of the college, they always end up working closely with him or her. Students, parents, and faculty with a direct complaint or problem about the dean or the student affairs program often take it directly to the president. No one, especially a president, likes to be caught by surprise. A dean of students should thus keep the president well informed about a potential problem, provide an explanation of what has happened, and recommend a means of resolving the issue. If the dean does not report to the president, it is important to work out with the supervisor the means by which information will be shared with the president, so it does not appear as if the dean is trying to go over the supervisor's head.

Always try to remember that one of the chief jobs of a dean of students is to keep problems off the desk of the president. Whenever possible, advise the president to refer the problems back to the dean's office for resolution. Regardless of the reporting structure, it is very important that a dean of students know the president well and that the president fully understands and supports the philosophy and approach of the student affairs program. The president will be required to defend the program and decisions made by the dean of students on countless occasions to students, faculty, staff, and parents. The president should know the program and the dean so well that given the facts of a situation he or she can predict what actions will be taken.

PRESIDENT'S CABINET

Most small, private, liberal arts college presidents will have a weekly meeting with the senior administrators, commonly called the president's cabinet or staff. If the dean reports directly to the president, he or she will automatically be a member of the cabinet. If the dean reports to a vice president, however, this is not a given. It is extremely important, if not crucial, for the dean of students to be a member of this group. As a senior officer in the institution and one who regularly has to explain and defend institutional actions to students and parents, it is essential to have first-hand knowledge and understanding of the basis for the college's decisions. Further, a key part of the dean of students' role is to represent student needs to the primary decision-makers of the college, a difficult achievement when working through an intermediary. Problems and challenges in all areas of the college will be discussed in these meetings, offering an opportunity to get to know and understand the entire institution. The more knowledgeable one is about the college, of course, the more effective the dean can be.

It is important to recognize and respect the confidential nature of many of the discussions which will take place in the president's cabinet meetings. When defending or explaining actions taken by this group, it is important to understand what can and cannot be shared with others. The dean's effectiveness in appropriately representing the decisions and actions of the president's cabinet to other constituencies will play a large part in determining how influential the dean will be in the cabinet.

TRUSTEES

I have listed the trustees in this part because they are legally the administrative officers of the college. The role and function of the trustees of a college vary widely from one college to another. The traditional roles of the trustees at the small, private, liberal arts college are to: (a) set the broad mission and goals of the institution, (b) ensure its financial health, and (c) hire and supervise the president of the institution. Trustees normally are not involved in the day-to-day operation of the institution, nor in setting its general policies and procedures. These responsibilities are delegated by the trustees to the president. Due to this, one would assume that the trustees would not have a great deal of involvement with the student affairs operations, unless those operations were somehow not supporting the broad missions and goals of the institution. It is rarely, however, quite this simple.

At institutions with strong religious missions where there is explicit concern for the moral aspects of student conduct, the trustees often become directly involved in social policies and regulations relating to students. At non-sectarian liberal arts colleges, some boards of trustees have become quite involved in the daily operations of the college, often due to perceived or real problems of mismanagement on the part of the administration. Trustees have generally reserved for themselves the authority to make final decisions on all major building projects, often even who will be retained as the architect and general contractor. They will undoubtedly be involved in any building project relating to student affairs.

A dean must clearly understand and remember one thing about the trustees: The only person who reports to them is the president of the college, and most presidents tend to be somewhat protective of this relationship. It is not appropriate for a dean to contact a trustee or to establish a close relationship with one, without the knowledge and consent of the president. The dean should have a clear understanding of what the president considers the dean's role with the trustees to be and of how the president wishes the dean to carry out this role.

The trustees are often a highly interesting and competent group of people who are enjoyable to work with and to know, and who usually have a strong commitment to the college. They are often the primary source of the college's external funding. Trustees want to feel they are part of the college, so they enjoy getting to know students, faculty, and staff. Although there is nothing inappropriate about the dean getting to know the trustees and talking with them about the college, some caution should be exercised. It is not unheard of for trustees to try to solicit information from deans about the president, or try to get deans' views on issues on which the president has already expressed an opinion or taken a position. Most presidents will not appreciate learning that members of their staff have been voicing opinions to the trustees contrary to their own.

COLLEGE COMMITTEES

No monograph written about higher education administration could be complete without mentioning committees. In no other organization are committees used and abused to the degree that they are in colleges and universities. I once calculated that a full one-third of my time as a dean of students was spent in committee meetings, a calculation that motivated my most serious thoughts about leaving the profession and has convinced me that I would never want to be a congressman.

Committees have proliferated in higher education because they are used for educational purposes although they are also used as a delaying technique almost as often as a decision-making tool. With students, the committee is actually a good educational tool: for example, when highly opinionated students serve on a committee and must rationally discuss favored proposals, their implementation, and possible indirect problems, they often become some of the most rational and reasonable people in the college community. For this reason, I have always appointed students to a majority of seats on student life committees. This gives the committees and their decisions much greater credibility with students, and helps attract good students for the committee. A committee decision also cannot simply be written off as an administrative ultimatum when students are in the majority.

Committee on Student Life
It is essential to have a committee composed of students, faculty, and staff, with students in the majority, to deal with social policies and regulations. Students should be appointed by the student government association, staff members by the dean of students, and faculty members by the president or academic dean, in consultation with the dean of students. The latter is especially important because if the faculty itself makes the faculty appointments, there is a tendency to appoint faculty members to this committee whom they do not wish to appoint to faculty committees. It is a fact of life that students tend to listen to and trust faculty members more than they do administrators, so good faculty members are a necessary component of this committee. If the appointment method for faculty poses insurmountable political problems, another alternative is to have the students nomi-

nate them. Students tend to be very good about picking the faculty members who will work best with them on committees.

For many reasons, it is highly inadvisable to leave the promulgation of social policies and regulations solely to the student government association: it is too political a body; it cannot take the time necessary to thoroughly explore issues; it does not always have easy access to needed institutional data; and, most important, it does not represent the needs of the entire institution. As I earlier suggested, a college is not a political democracy, and it should not be one. It is an educational institution, and social policies and regulations have a direct effect upon the educational process. Student affairs staff and, especially, the faculty, should have a direct role in deciding these issues. I also advise that the dean of students act as a non-voting chair of this committee.

The committee on student life should be responsible for making recommendations concerning all social policies and regulations directly to the president of the college. Because of this, it is advisable for the president of the student government association to be one of the student members of the committee, to assure that the student government will be directly represented in the making of social policy, and to enable the student government president to explain effectively the actions of the committee to the student senate. It also lessens the possibility that this committee and the student government will be at odds with each other. I would also recommend that there be a formal procedure by which the student government can challenge committee policy recommendations.

Housing Committee

I advise having a separate housing committee, particularly on a primarily residential campus, with a composition similar to the student life committee. Housing issues are very important to students, and for this reason, they should have a majority voice on this committee. The director of housing can serve as the non-voting chair, and at least one resident director should be a member.

The housing committee should be responsible for recommending all housing policies to the dean of students, including the gender make-up of the residence halls, special group living situations, vandalism and damage policies, security issues, furnishings and renovations, and space utilization. The committee can also make recommendations to the student life committee for social policies and regulations which they think would improve campus housing. All housing committee decisions would be recommendations to the dean of students.

Other Committees

One of the primary reasons for having committees in student affairs is to involve students directly and meaningfully in the student affairs programs. If this is done effectively, students gain more of a sense of ownership of these programs and student participation in them increases. Every student affairs program, such as career services, health services, multicultural affairs, international student affairs, and counseling services, should have an advisory committee composed of students, staff, and, whenever possible, faculty. The director of the unit should chair the committee and bear primary responsibility for bringing issues to it for consideration. One task of the committee would be assisting the director in carrying out regular evaluations of the services offered by the student affairs unit. The committee also can be an effective political ally in representing the office or program to the rest of the campus, and it can give the director greater credibility when making recommendations for change and requests for further funding and staff.

As was discussed in the section on the faculty, a dean of students should seriously consider creating a faculty advisory committee for the student affairs office. The dean can chair this committee, select the faculty to be on it, and make certain that members understand that this is an advisory, not a policy-making, committee. In selecting the faculty members, the dean might attempt to select men and women who represent various faculty attitudes and to try to get the participation of at least one of the most severe faculty critics of the student affairs programs. Faculty members critical of the program can explain and defend their criticisms in front of the committee rather than privately. If it is effective, this committee can also be helpful in representing the student affairs program and its needs to the rest of the college community.

It is often advisable for the dean of students to take the initiative in establishing committees or work groups in areas and on issues that are likely to become controversial on the campus. Examples of some of these are women's issues, multicultural concerns, gay/lesbian/bisexual concerns, and non-traditional student concerns. By establishing mechanisms that allow such topics to be openly discussed within the official channels of the college, problems can sometimes be resolved before their coming to a bitter and confrontational head.

Ad Hoc Committees

By an *ad hoc* committee, I am referring to committees which have no official standing on their own, report to another standing committee or administrator, are limited in their scope of responsibilities to the immediate issue assigned to them, and whose existence ends when the issue being addressed is resolved. An *ad hoc* committee can be especially useful for conducting research and making recommendations on a particularly complicated issue, for example, an *ad hoc* committee created by the committee on student life to study the issue of alcohol consumption and possession on campus and recommend alternative policies which the college could adopt. A small *ad hoc* committee can meet more easily and more often than can the full committee; gather the detailed legal information needed; design, administer, and compile data from questionnaires; and spend the focused time necessary to study a complicated issue. The *ad hoc* committee would then present the information it had gathered and its recommendations to the full committee on student life for its consideration. An added benefit is that all of the members of the *ad hoc* committee do not have to be members of the committee on student life, allowing for a broader participation in the process and enabling people with specific knowledge or skills who may not be on the parent committee to participate. In the charter establishing any committee, the dean of students should insert a clause allowing it to establish *ad hoc* committees to help it with its responsibilities.

In spite of my initial complaints about committees in higher education, it is apparent that not only are they here to stay, but they can fulfill some very valuable functions. There are some skills — some would call them tricks — involved in making effective use of committees.

When establishing student committees, always try to appoint the dean, or the student affairs administrator responsible for the area in which the committee is working, as chair of the committee. Elected chairpersons tend to be remarkably inconsistent in their effectiveness. Many do not have the necessary organizational skills, do not know what agenda to establish, do not know what information the committee needs so that it can make effective decisions, and do not have ready access to the required information. The student affairs administrator responsible for the area the committee is working on will be committed to the committee's success, and if he or she is made a non-voting chair, many potential objections will be overcome.

I always volunteer to write the initial draft of any committee proposal, and if it is my own proposal, I always present it in the form of a written draft. The initial draft almost always forms the framework not only for the committee discussion but for the final accepted proposal, so the person who writes this draft has a tremendous influence on the direction the committee will take in its final action. This simple truth was revealed to me the first time I was faced with a draft proposal with which I substantially disagreed. To get an original draft of a proposal completely rewritten on the floor of a committee is virtually impossible. The draft will almost always be modified rather than substantially changed.

Although this may seem to contradict the paragraph above, try to have faith in the committee process and support committee decisions. If I wish to have effective student life committees and want their decisions to be respected on the campus, I must support the committee process, even when my own position is not accepted by the committee. There will always be another day and a committee composed of different people. Sometimes I have had to wait 10 years for the right group of committee members to be selected. Patience is a quality which a dean needs in large quantity.

HIRING, SUPERVISION, AND EVALUATION OF STAFF

Since student affairs is a staff-intensive program, the hiring, supervision, and evaluation of professional staff is one of the most important responsibilities of a dean of students.

The Hiring Process

Directors of human resources probably cringe when they consider the hiring processes used in higher education. Our searches are time consuming, grueling, and often lack the objectivity desired by human resources managers. It is not unusual for candidates to spend two days being interviewed by people from nearly every constituent group on the campus. Most human resources directors would prefer us to interview a candidate for no more than a few hours and with no more than one to three people conducting the interview. They would prefer that all candidates be asked exactly the same questions and the questions be strictly confined to objective issues concerning the specific job skills required for the position. The supervisor would then decide to whom the contract would be offered.

In my experience, few colleges conform to these guidelines. A collegial culture is very different from a corporate one. The ability to work with and relate to very different constituent groups, the fit with institutional values and purposes, and the need to have different constituent groups committed to the person hired are very important in college searches. Because our interviewing processes are quite different from those used in many other settings, we should be aware of the need to explain our hiring practices and their rationale carefully to candidates from outside of higher education. The search committee concept, in particular, is rarely found outside of higher education.

There is no such a thing as a perfect hiring process. Whether someone who interviews well can also do the job well cannot be known until the new employee has worked on campus for several months. This is not to say, however, that some interviewing procedures are not better than others or that different hiring processes are not appropriate for different levels of employment. I will outline some of my recommendations based primarily on many years of conducting searches. Each dean, however, must find procedures in which he or she has confidence and which conform to specific institutional guidelines.

Search Committees

Many colleges use search committees composed of students, faculty, and staff. Often search committees are formed due to historical practice rather than because real thought has been given to their justification and purpose. The methodology and duties of search committees differ from campus to campus. A common model provides the dean with a passive role until the final decision has been made. The committee reads the *vitae*, completes reference checks, conducts telephone interviews, decides which candidates to bring to campus, participates in campus interviews, and then recommends to the dean the candidate(s) who should be hired.

I have not been able to find the historical origins of search committees, but most likely they lie in faculty searches in highly collegial and egalitarian institutions where straight line supervision does not exist. To me, search committees make little sense in student affairs and I recommend against their use. Too often search processes on small college campuses are as much political as they are an objective means of selecting the most qualified applicant. Too often people are selected to be on search teams based on their political constituencies rather than for their knowledge, experience, and ability to interview and assess candidates' abilities.

The dean, or the direct supervisor of the position being filled, should be responsible for the search process. Such an administrator will ultimately be accountable for whomever is hired and will usually have the most knowledge and experience in the search and hiring process. As much as is possible, politics should be taken out of the search process.

I personally believe in having a rather large number of people, particularly student affairs staff members and students, interview candidates. It is useful to have the interviews conducted in a variety of settings, such as one-to-one, groups, luncheons, and dinners. When appropriate, it can be very useful to have the candidates put on a presentation or conduct a short workshop that might be typical of those they would be required to do on the job.

Internal Promotions
Prior to considering any internal promotion, the affirmative action officer of the institution must be consulted to assure that such a promotion can be done within the institution's guidelines. The potential for internal promotion without an external search is a powerful motivational tool that some institutions have given up in the interest of affirmative action. This is unfortunate. Often there is no better method to predict an individual's performance at a particular institution than their proving their competence on the job. Also, putting internal candidates through the harrowing process of an open search can be damaging to morale, both theirs and the rest of the staff's. I strongly believe in affirmative action and have witnessed its effectiveness in helping to bring more diverse groups to our campuses, but its goals need to be balanced against the legitimate need of an institution to be able to retain excellent staff through internal promotions. The opening resulting from a promotion can be filled through an affirmative action ex-

ternal search. It is worth the effort to put policies into place that allow for internal promotions for exceptional staff.

Internal Searches

Internal searches, as opposed to internal promotions, can be used when there is more than one person at the college who has the qualifications to perform the duties and when internal searches are allowed by the institution's affirmative action guidelines. Internal searches must be conducted with great care and sensitivity or they can be very hard on candidates and their institutional colleagues. If not conducted well, they can tear a staff apart. Procedural equity is all important. All candidates must be treated the same by all involved in the search process, and all candidates should be privy to identical information about the position.

Do not allow a staff member to become a candidate for an internal search unless the person is a viable candidate. An internal search is not the time to see if a person can prove himself or herself. It is inappropriate to use the search process as a way of avoiding an honest discussion with the staff member about why he or she is not qualified for the position.

In open searches, I normally arrange a meeting of all the people who participate in the interviews to discuss the candidates' strengths and weaknesses; during internal searches, I forego this process. At a small college, where everyone personally knows the candidates, this can cause real problems among the staff. Some interviewers may not be willing to be completely honest due to fears that their opinions may get back to the candidates. Confidentiality can be a real problem. Instead, I ask all persons involved in the interviews to fill out written evaluation forms and also invite them to speak with me individually if they would like to do so.

Resident Director Searches

Although I normally advise that the supervisor for the position being filled make the final decision as to whom the contract should be offered, the exception to this is in searches for resident directors. Due to the position's live-in nature and the close interaction resident directors have with students, these searches should be conducted somewhat differently. Resident directors must be able to relate effectively with students, and students must support the person hired. Students will be much more likely to demonstrate a commitment to the success of new resident directors if they have been allowed to play a major role in the selection process. For these reasons, I use a very open and democratic search process for resident director positions, where students and staff mutually decide to whom contracts should be offered.

Supervision and Evaluation

The supervision of staff is one of the most important and most time-consuming functions of a dean of students. One trap many deans at small liberal arts colleges fall into is having everyone in student affairs report directly to them. This situation can be reinforced by the desire of many of the staff to report directly to the dean. The demands placed on the dean of students, however, both to be available to any and all students and to manage a host of complicated administrative programs can become overwhelming. Good associate deans should be given supervisory responsibility for some of the staff and the programs they direct. For example, an associate dean for academic support programs could also supervise the career services office and the counseling center.

How often the dean has regular supervisory meetings with individual staff members will vary depending upon their function, experience, and length of time at the college. I have found it best to have a standing meeting once a week with staff I supervise. Extra time and attention may be needed by new staff members, especially those taking on difficult assignments, and young staff members who have had little experience in their new duties. In these instances, I encourage staff members to come in and see me more often if they feel the need to do so.

Deans have an obligation to explain their supervisory style to those they supervise. For example, I like to throw out ideas to staff members in order to have them analyzed and critiqued. Unless I explain this to my staff and encourage them to respond, they are usually very reluctant to criticize the ideas of a supervisor. The purpose of the supervisory meetings with staff must also be clear. Is, for example, the agenda of these meetings set by the concerns of the staff members or by those of the dean?

One component of good supervision is direct and honest feedback. If a staff member has made a mistake or done something with which I disagree, I try to bring this to their attention and discuss it immediately. It is not appropriate to wait for a year-end evaluation to point out problems.

Staff members should understand clearly how independently they are expected to work and what the limits of their authority are. Do I want to discuss situations with the person before they act, just want to be kept informed of what they are doing, or should my involvement be based on the specific character of a particular situation?

The evaluation system for all student affairs administrators should include input from students, staff, and faculty. One method is to have a thorough evaluation for each staff member after the end of his or her first year and then every third year thereafter, where students, staff, and faculty are sent evaluation forms concerning the employee. The names are taken from the staff member's appointment calendar and from the list of students on committees and organizations with which the staff member works. Those completing the evaluation forms have the option of signing or not signing their names. The forms are returned to the staff member's immediate supervisor, who collates the results and shares them with the staff member. Because this is such a time-consuming process, I recommend having this thorough evaluation only every three years. This also avoids overevaluation which can cause staff to think they are constantly under scrutiny. In the intervening years, the evaluation can be done by the supervisor.

Supervision of professional residence hall staff can sometimes be a challenge. These are usually young people fresh out of graduate programs, filled with new theories and a great deal of idealism. This is what makes them interesting; they tend to have a rejuvenating effect on older staff members. On the other hand, they are often quite naive in their enthusiasm and idealism and, like most young people, are apt to be impatient. Evaluation of resident directors is essential to maintaining a good program. At both Grinnell and Reed Colleges, students have been heavily involved in the evaluation process for these positions. Because the students and the student staff are the primary constituents of the resident director, his or her ability to work with them effectively is of paramount importance. New staff members coming into the small college may make mistakes initially, due to their lack of familiarity with the college's unique culture. For this reason, a short initial evaluation should be done after the first four to six weeks on the job. This evaluation can be done by the student resident adviser staff. The resident director and the students involved in the evaluation process must understand clearly that its purpose is to provide constructive feedback to the resident director early on to assist him or her achieve suc-

achieve success. The resident director's supervisor should then meet with the resident director to review thoroughly the results of the student evaluations and to add his or her observations of the resident director's job performance in as supportive a way as possible with the goal of improving performance. In the early spring, a thorough evaluation should be completed by a resident director's student staff, all the students or a statistically valid random sample of the students who live in the halls for which the resident director is responsible, and all other student affairs staff who have significant work relationships with the resident director. This evaluation determines whether to offer a contract for the next year. For this reason, it must be carried out early enough in the spring so that the resident director is able to look for other employment if the decision is negative.

Supervision, while difficult, can be one of the most rewarding roles of a dean. Watching and helping staff members to mature, learn, improve, and achieve self-confidence is very satisfying, as is observing them go into more responsible roles and achieve professional success. Due to the level of my own responsibility and time commitments, I must often work with students through other staff members. They represent me and the program for which I am responsible; how well they do this is crucial to the program's success. Time spent on supervision is rarely wasted.

LEGAL COUNSEL

More than 20 years ago, when I first became a dean of students, I would only use legal counsel, on the average, a couple of times a year. I am now consulting with college attorneys at least once a week, largely due to the increased legal requirements imposed by state and federal governments and heightened concern about risk management and liability. Legal counsel seems to have all but taken over in the area of personnel problems.

Small liberal arts colleges have a variety of arrangements for legal counsel. Some very few have their own in-house counsel. Most contract with a law firm or firms to provide legal assistance. For colleges located in rural areas, it is not uncommon for their primary attorney to be located in a nearby city. Many colleges use different attorneys for different issues. For example, a college may use one attorney for issues dealing with contract law, another for personnel issues, and yet another for issues concerning risk management.

My advice to deans of students is to get to know your attorneys and get to know their professional and personal characteristics, styles, and values well. I spend a considerable amount of time with them on complicated, important, and sometimes emotionally charged issues, and I have found that when we are in tense situations, it is good for us to have gotten to know each other in advance.

One of the most crucial lessons to learn is to distinguish between two situations: when lawyers are detailing what the law requires and when they are giving legal advice. There is a world of difference between the two situations. I have been put in the unfortunate position of thinking my attorney was saying that I was legally required to do something I did not wish to do and, only later, after I had carried out the action, did I learn that he was merely *advising* me on what to do. The actions I had taken were against my better professional judgment and I lived to regret them. I have found that it is not good practice to allow attorneys to assume my responsibilities for me.

It is also very important to educate attorneys concerning the particular culture and ethos of a college, particularly if they have not had experience working in higher education. They need to know and understand the context in which I work if they are going to be able to give me appropriate advice. What works in the corporate world often does not work in the collegiate world. In particular, college attorneys must be educated about the governance and decision-making process at the college. If they are not familiar with colleges, they may assume that a vice president or dean has much more authority to make decisions arbitrarily and take actions than is, in fact, the case. If I am working with an attorney who has not had much experience working in higher education, I encourage him or her to join the Association of Student Judicial Affairs, read its periodicals, and attend its conferences.

Deans must also keep themselves current with the laws of higher education and the requirements of new legislation; one way to do this is by forming a real partnership with the college's attorneys. I have even attended law in higher education conferences with my college attorney and both of us found this to be very beneficial. Not only did we come to share a more common knowledge base, but we were able to get to know each other much better. Attorneys are going to remain an important player in student affairs, and it is crucial that deans learn how to work effectively with them.

RENOVATION AND CONSTRUCTION OF STUDENT LIFE BUILDINGS

Renovation may not be a daily concern of the dean of students, but anyone who is a dean of students for a very long period of time will be involved in at least one and probably several renovation projects. Student affairs buildings are usually renovated only once every 30 to 40 years, so when the opportunity arises, it is crucial that the task be done well. The example of the renovation or construction of residence halls will demonstrate some of the issues a dean needs to address during any type of renovation and will suggest a methodology to use in managing the process.

Most of the residence halls on small campuses were built at least 20 to 40 years ago and need major work due to deferred maintenance. A dean who goes blindly into the renovation of these buildings not only loses a golden opportunity but may also do a drastic disservice to students for years to come.

Residence Hall Renovations or Construction

Environmental issues such as size, location and design of lounges, hallways, study areas, student rooms, and bathrooms have a tremendous influence on how students live with each other and upon the quality of their interactions. If this seems an exaggeration, simply spend some time on a floor where all of the rooms are singles with their own bathrooms without a public lounge. Then spend some time on a floor where the rooms are singles, doubles, and triples, with common bathrooms and a public lounge. The first setting will seem to be uninhabited, with many students not knowing the names of other floor residents, and residents rarely getting together with groups of students from the floor do anything. In the second setting, students will be moving up and down the hallways and will be in the lounge, with most knowing each other's names and backgrounds, and with groups participating in activities together.

Before any design work is done on the renovation or construction of a residence hall, a clear statement of goals must be determined. An ex-

ample of goals I have used is given below, with the implications for renovations given for each of these goals.

■ *Goal:* To have a residence hall where new students and upperclass
students are intermingled.

Renovation or Construction Implications: Needs a variety of rooms.
Doubles assigned to new students and singles, with triples and suites, or
both, to attract upperclass students.

■ *Goal:* To have halls that can be used for either single-sex or coed
living situations.

Renovation or Construction Implications: Needs to have two bathrooms on each floor for privacy of the sexes and doors at the end of each
hallway which can be locked, so security will already be in place if the
floor is used for single-sex living.

■ *Goal:* To have students identify with each other and participate in
both floor and hall activities.

Renovation or Construction Implications: Needs a social space on
each floor, a residence hall lounge large enough to accommodate all of the
residents, plus invited guests. Needs kitchens for students to prepare snacks
and light meals.

■ *Goal:* To make the residence hall a place where students can study
as well as socialize.

Renovation or Construction Implications: Needs excellent acousti-
cal treatment of student rooms and hallways. Hallways will probably have
to be carpeted. Adequate study rooms must be provided, with wiring in-
stalled for computer use. Furnishings for a variety of study situations will
have to be purchased. Consideration should be given to providing small
computer laboratories within the residence halls.

■ *Goal:* Have as many upperclass students as possible, including
juniors and seniors, live in the residence halls.

Renovation or Construction Implications: Must meet the increasing
need for privacy desired by many upperclass students by providing single
rooms at a moderate price. Consider the option of suites with single rooms
and cooking facilities.

■ *Goal:* Have security for the building, its furnishings, and the occu-
pants, while maintaining maximum access to the building by nonresident

student friends. Hold residents collectively liable for damages to public areas.

Renovation or Construction Implications: Must devise a system where students who have legitimate reasons can easily enter the building yet which offers adequate protection of the property for which the college is holding students responsible, as well as adequate protection of the residents. Needs security telephones externally located at building entrances, so friends can quickly and easily call a resident to let them in the hall and security telephones strategically located within the halls, so students can call 911 if they need help.

■ *Goal:* To give students privacy in bathrooms without unreasonable construction and maintenance costs.

Renovation or Construction Implications: Cannot give private bathrooms to each room, due to construction and maintenance costs; consider sinks in each room, to give more space in public bathroom. Do not have community showers; design showers which have private dressing rooms. Have at least one shower for every five students. Make the bathrooms as appealing as possible, yet easy to maintain.

The process described is very simple and practical because the goals are very clearly stated. It is surprising how many residence hall renovations or construction projects are designed by trying to give something to everyone and ending up with a building which cannot support the desired living goals.

Renovations and construction projects require an architect, and the dean of students should do everything possible to have a direct influence on choosing this person. A very competent architect who has prior experience with residence halls or multiple living units, who is not out to create a monument to him or herself, and who has a knowledge of and appreciation for the necessity of having function be the final determining factor in design or renovation of the halls should be sought. The ideal situation involves an understanding from the outset that function will determine design, and that I, as the dean of students, will be responsible for determining function.

A bit of simply acquired technical skill can help one immensely in carrying out these responsibilities. I have found it invaluable to gain competence in reading architectural blueprints and a basic understanding of architectural and construction terms, as well as to develop a good feel for the use of architectural space. With this knowledge, I can sit down with a building's blueprints and sketch out rough designs that will fulfill the renovation's intended function. When I then meet with the architect, we can work together on the final plans and drawings. Architects do not have to be the enemy if you work closely with them. They are creative people who, once they understand the desired goal, may be able to offer novel and effective design options for meeting that goal.

A dean of students also needs to have a basic understanding of mechanical systems: plumbing, heating, and wiring. One of the biggest problems in residence halls is that they are uncomfortable. The room is too hot or too cold, the shower water either scalding or icy, with the student having little, if any, control over the temperatures. These problems can be resolved when the residence hall is renovated. Good insulation, zone heating controls, and good plumbing systems are readily available.

I systematically ask for and get student ideas about the renovations. The most useful information is garnered through discussions rather than questionnaires, or, at least, questionnaires that are supplemented by discussions. Students should be mainly asked questions about function rather than design details. They can be a wonderful source of information about how they live in and use a building, about its assets and liabilities. When students are asked about design details, however, the result is a confusing array of individual preferences. It is important to remember, moreover, that the final responsibility for the design falls on the dean of students, who with the help and assistance of others, has worked out the program concept that sets goals for what the residence halls are to accomplish beyond providing students with individual comfort. The halls have to be designed to fit the learning and living programs for the next 20 to 30 years, not the individual desires of the present generation of students.

ADVICE TO NEW DEANS

Deans of students, whether moving into their first deanship, new to the profession from the ranks of the faculty, or new to an institution, face particular challenges and opportunities. The first and most important task is to get to know and establish a relationship with the president, who in most cases will also be the supervisor. Even when I have worked at the institution prior to becoming a dean, my new role has meant a new relationship with the president. This relationship is vital to future success. Several issues should be discussed, preferably over a period of time:

■ What does the president see as the role of the dean with students, faculty, other administrative offices, and the trustees?

■ How does the president prefer to work with the dean; what authority will be delegated; on what issues should the dean consult with the president prior to taking action; on what issues should the dean regularly keep the president informed; and what should be the dean's relationship with the trustees and how should he or she work with them?

■ What philosophy of student affairs, if any, does the president have? How does it conform to the dean's and, if it does not, how will the differences be worked out?

■ What are the weaknesses of the present student affairs programs and staff and what needs to be done to make improvements?

When new to a college, I have found it essential to immerse myself in learning its history and culture. Small colleges are unique and pride themselves in being so. A dean of students must be particularly sensitive to the ethos of the institution and to both the written and unwritten rules by which it is governed. I have gone to the college archives and read everything I could get my hands on, including faculty, trustee, and student senate minutes, past student newspapers, governance documents, and historical documents written about the college.

It is very important to learn the language of the college. Most small colleges have peculiarities concerning language, sometimes even in spelling when there is more than one correct choice. One should be especially attentive to attitudes toward student affairs jargon, which is looked down upon in some institutions. Even when this is not so, it is often advisable, particularly when speaking with faculty, to use lay terms rather than professional language.

Set up individual appointments with every student affairs staff member and use the appointments first to listen and learn and, second, to let them get to know you, your philosophy, and your expectations. If at all possible, take considerable time before making or proposing any major changes in either the student affairs organization or college policies. Change is threatening at any time, but can be particularly threatening when initiated by someone who is new to the college.

Try to get to know faculty members and the academic dean as quickly as possible. At most small institutions, faculty members are at the college's core and have the most long-term influence over its direction. Their support for student affairs will be crucial to a dean's success. The support of a strong academic dean can be invaluable in gaining the respect of the faculty. It takes time, however, to get to know the faculty. They must be sought out, and this is not always best done in a formal manner. Try not to miss any opportunity for faculty contact.

New Deans from the Faculty

New deans of students who come from the faculty often have real challenges and adjustments to make in order to be successful, and this arrangement deserves special mention. The first shock to a new dean from the faculty is often the workload itself. This is not to imply that faculty do not work hard, but the life of a college administrator is very different from that of a faculty member. Few faculty members genuinely understand and appreciate this until they make the transition. The first shock is often the amount of control over their lives that they lose. Their secretary, their calendar, and countless meetings and appointments take over their lives to a degree rare among the faculty.

The second shock is often discovering how little authority they have. Many times faculty members do not realize the amount of authority they exercise on a daily basis in the classroom and over the curriculum, and they are not used to the amount of consultation and time it takes to get things done within the administration. New deans from the faculty must quickly realize and adapt to this reality: the dean of students must be a person who believes in and is capable of using influence and persuasion rather than unilateral authority. This requires several skills and characteristics, the main ones being patience, oral and written competence, knowledge of individual and group behavior, the ability to quickly diagnose complex social and structural problems, the ability to admit mistakes, and a strong sense of self-confidence. Ultimately, the only true power of deans of students is the ability to persuade and influence, and this requires that they be trusted by all the campus constituents. New deans coming from the faculty sometimes stumble badly and early, by not recognizing the limits on their authority. The first mistake many of these new deans make is taking an arbitrary action or stance without proper consultation or the proper use of the established decision-making processes.

The other danger for a dean from the faculty is that of assuming he or she knows everything about an institution in which they have taught for many years. Student and administrative culture and practices are often very different from those of the faculty, even within the same institution. One simple example is the vast difference that often exists between the collegial relationships faculty share with each other and the hierarchical relationships that exist within administrations, particularly those between supervisors and staff. Faculty are used to arguing and debating with each other on an equal and often confrontational basis. This is usually not the norm in a supervisory staff relationship, and, even when it approximates it, there is always the unspoken reality of a difference in power. Collegiality, in the faculty sense of that word, often does not exist within administrative structures. New deans coming from the faculty should take the time to learn about administrative and student cultures. Students often treat staff in a different manner from faculty, and this can take quite an adjustment.

The new dean coming from the faculty should seek out deans at similar institutions who also came from faculty positions and spend some time with them. They can help the new dean understand some of the transitions that will have to be made as the new role is assumed. New deans should immediately become involved in state, regional, and national professional organizations, so they can meet as many other deans as possible and learn from them. If the college belongs to a consortium of similar colleges, this organization can provide an ideal site for meeting peers at other institutions and seeking their assistance.

I have discussed the pitfalls which new deans coming directly from the faculty might face, but they also have some very real advantages. Relationships with the faculty can be very helpful in gaining an understanding and a greater acceptance for the role of student affairs. Prior in-depth knowledge of the institution can help to avoid many of the unintended errors made by new deans coming from outside of the institution. Usually loyalty and commitment to the institution are already established and have been demonstrated in the past.

Regardless, however, of which path is taken to become the dean of students, expect the first few years to be very busy ones with long hours of work. As a new dean I found I had to do my homework well, as fewer errors are tolerated of a dean than is the case with many lower-level positions, and the errors I did make were open to a great deal of public scrutiny.

CONCLUSION

By now, it should be apparent that this manuscript is a personal statement about what I have learned and what I believe about the position of the dean of students and the student affairs program at the small college. Fundamentally, I want to convey an optimistic belief in the basic goodness of human nature, particularly that of students. Mine is a belief based on the premise that if we treat students like responsible adults, most of them will respond as such and take greater advantage of the educational opportunities the college offers. This is not, however, just a belief. It is a personal and professional truth discovered through many years of working day and night with students and student affairs programs.

I have observed that students respond positively to being given control of their own lives, residence halls, and organizations. This is not to say that there have not been problems and that it has not been a constant struggle. When it comes to humans, there is no such thing as a perfect social, much less educational, structure. Good programs are fluid, constantly in the process of being fine-tuned and changed. As I stated previously, the basic human nature of students and the human development problems they face change little over the years. While I believe this to be true, it is also true that the world from which students come and the world they face often changes quite drastically. New threats, challenges, and opportunities will always face new generations of college students, and this has required me to adjust not only many of the topics and materials in the educational programs I offer in student affairs but also the ways in which I work with students.

The best programs, however, build naturally upon themselves and are based upon premises which rarely change. These are the programs that become so incorporated into the college's ethos that the values of the program are passed down from one generation of students to the next. They are so well-defined that when a stranger comes on campus and asks about them, the dean of students, the chair of the faculty, the president of the college, the president of the student government association, and random students in the residence halls can provide consistent answers, even using the same key phrases and words to describe them. They fit the institution, its traditions, its mission, and the students they serve. They are programs that help students to be academically successful and take full advantage of the college.

I have often been asked by younger colleagues in the field whether, if given the choice, I would choose to be a dean of students all over again. I can very truthfully answer in the affirmative. I have found student affairs to be a tremendously challenging and exciting profession which has brought few dull moments in over 25 years of practice. It has required me to learn a great deal about individual and group behavior, has taught me remarkable tolerance for what often appears to be irrational and inexplicable behavior, has taught me patience far beyond what I thought was possible, has forced me to examine and learn more about myself, and has helped me to appreciate the value of knowing and appreciating diverse people.

The dean of students position at the small, private, liberal arts college is certainly not, however, a job for everyone. Due to its size and its emphasis upon individual attention, the environment is an intensely personal one. There is no door thick enough or strong enough to hide behind. My professional, personal, and social life are often so intertwined that it is difficult to tell one from the other. Nearly my entire life has become immersed in the colleges for which I have worked, their students, their staff, and their faculty. I have found very little opportunity to become an eight-to-five o'clock working person who leaves my professional life at the office. Depending on one's personality, this can be a very exciting total experience or an incredibly draining one. If a person does not like confrontation, conflict, mediating people's problems, having their beliefs challenged constantly, responding to emergencies at all hours of the day and night, and constantly struggling with their administrative colleagues over scarce resources, then being a dean of students is probably not their cup of tea.

There are, however, tremendous rewards that go along with being a dean. Students are remarkably interesting people to work with and are genuinely appreciative of the help they are given. The challenges they present will force deans to grow, personally and intellectually. As stated earlier, my beliefs have not been unexamined; the students, the faculty, and my own staff have not allowed them to be. Student affairs staffs are an interesting and diverse group of caring people who appreciate good supervision and have constantly brought new concerns and concepts to my attention. Faculty are some of the most interesting and intellectually stimulating people with whom one could ever work and they make wonderful colleagues. There is also tremendous satisfaction to be gained from creating and implementing a program that truly enhances students' education and helps them to become mature, responsible adults. There have been many instances when I and my staff have saved lives, been responsible for helping students to be able to finish their college programs, and have prevented capable young people from leaving the college feeling as if they were failures. The challenges and problems are many, but so are the rewards.

References

Astin, A.W. (1993). *What matters in college*. San Francisco: Jossey-Bass Publisher, Inc.

Bloland, P.A., Stamatakos, L.C., and Russell, R.R. (1994). *Reform in student affairs*. Greensboro, NC: ERIC Counseling and Student Services Clearing House. (ERIC Document Reproduction Service No. ED 366 822).

Chickering, A.W. (1974). *Commuting versus resident students*. San Francisco: Jossey-Bass Publisher, Inc.

Chickering, A.W., and Reisser, L. (1993). *Education and identity* (2nd ed.). San Francisco: Jossey-Bass Publisher, Inc.

Kuh, G.D., Schuh, J.H., Whitt, E.J., and Associates (1991). *Involving colleges*. San Francisco: Jossey-Bass Publisher, Inc.

Maslow, A.H. (1971). *The farther reaches of human nature*. NY: Viking.

Pascarella, E.T., and Terenzini, P.T. (1991). *How college affects students*. San Francisco: Jossey-Bass Publisher, Inc.

Pavela, G. (1985). *The dismissal of students with mental disorders.* Asheville, NC: College Administration Publications.

Pope, H.G., and Yurgelun-Scott, D. (1996). The residual cognitive effects of heavy marijuana use in college students. *Journal of the American Medical Association, 275,* 521-527.

Wilson, R.C., Gaff, J.G., Dienst, Evelyn R., Wood, L., and Bavry, J. (1975). *College professors and their impact on students.* NY: Wiley.

Whiteley, J.M., and Associates (1982). *Character development in college students.* Schenectady, NY: Character Research Press.

About the Author

JAMES S. TEDERMAN is vice president and dean of student services at Reed College in Portland, Oregon. He has degrees from Stanford University and the University of Nebraska. His administrative experience includes two years as a resident director, one year as an assistant dean and director of housing, one year as an associate dean of students, and 23 years as a vice president or dean of students.